THE
WORLD'S
GREATEST
LOVERS

THE
WORLD'S
GREATEST
LOVERS

Edited by
Margaret Nicholas

OCTOPUS BOOKS

First published in 1985 by Octopus Books

This edition published in 1997
by Chancellor Press,
an imprint of
Reed Consumer Books Limited
Michelin House, 81 Fulham Road
London SW3 6RB

Reprinted 1997

ISBN 1 85152 873 3

Printed and bound in Great Britain
by Cox & Wyman Ltd, Reading, Berkshire

Contents

Acknowledgements

With a book such as this, covering such a wide variety of characters, the author must draw much of her information from previous works. It would be impossible to mention all of them, but the author wishes to acknowledge, in particular, the following writers: John Masters: *Casanova* (Michael Joseph); William Gerhardi and Hugh Kingsmill: *The Casanova Fable* (Jarrolds London Ltd); Lothar Gunther Buchheim: *Picasso, A Pictorial Biography* (Thames and Hudson); Jean Paul Crespello: *Picasso and His Women* (Hodder and Stoughton); Francoise Gilot and Carlton Lake: *Life with Picasso* (Signet Books); Elizabeth Longford: *Lord Byron* (Hutchinson); Margot Strickland: *The Byron Women* (Peter Owen); Ernest Alfred Vizetelly: *Loves of the Poets* (Holden and Hardingham); Madeleine Bingham: *The Great Lover, Sir Herbert Beerbohm Tree* (Hamish Hamilton); Frances Donaldson: *The Actor Managers* (Weidenfeld and Nicolson); Frederick de Reichenberg: *Prince Metternich in Love and War* (Martin Secker); Barbara Cartland: *Metternich, The Passionate Diplomat* (Hutchinson); *Book of Love and Lovers* (Sphere Books); Jasper Ridley; *Lord Palmerston* (Constable); A.J.P. Taylor: *British Prime Ministers* (Allan Wingate); Dennis Judd: *Lord Palmerston* (Weidenfeld and Nicolson) and *Edward VII* (Macdonald and Janes); R.F. Delderfield: *Napoleon in Love* (Pan Books); Andre Maurois: *Napoleon* (Thames and Hudson); David Stacton: *The Bonapartes* (Hodder and Stoughton); Frances Elliot: *Roman Gossip* (John Murray); W.N.C. Carlton: *Pauline, Favourite Sister of Napoleon* (Thornton Butterworth); Joanna Richardson: *Sarah Bernhardt* (Weidenfeld and Nicolson) and *The Courtesans* (Weidenfeld and Nicolson); William Emboden: *Sarah Bernhardt* (MacMillan NY); Henry Knepler: *The Gilded Stage* (Constable); Ernle Bradford: *Cleopatra* (Hodder and Stoughton); E. Beresford Chancellor: *The Lives of the Rakes* (Phillip Allan and Co); Dulcie M. Ashdown: *Royal Paramours* (Robert Hale); Christopher Falkus: *Charles II* (Book Club Associates); Keith Middlemass: *Edward VII* (Book Club Associates); Desmond Seward: *Prince of the Renaissance, the Golden Life of Francois I* (MacMillan); R.J. Knecht: *Francois I* (Cambridge University Press); Hesketh Pearson: *Extraordinary People* (Heinemann); Frank Harris: *My Life and Loves* (W.H. Allen); C.G.L. Du Cann: *The Loves of George Bernard Shaw* (Arthur Barker); Margaret Shenfield: *Bernard Shaw* (Thames and Hudson); O.F. Morshead (Ed): *Everybody's Pepys* (G. Bell and Sons); Robert Latham (Ed): *The Illustrated Pepys* (Book Club Associates); Irving Shulman: *Rudolph Valentino* (Leslie Frewin); Michael Freedland: *Maurice Chevalier* (Arther Barker); James Harding: *Maurice Chevalier* (Secker and Warburg); Michael Harrison: *Fanfare of Strumpets* (W.H. Allen); Henry Blyth: *Skittles* (Rupert Hart-Davis); Charles Castle: *La Belle Otéro* (Michael Joseph).

The publishers would like to thank the following for their kind permission to reproduce the pictures used in this book: Topham Picture Library 17, 23, 41, 69, 157, 160; Mary Evans Picture Library 27, 29, 32, 42, 47, 48, 51, 59, 90, 99, 106, 109, 115, 122, 131, 167, 176, 190; Keystone Press Agency 62, 77, 80, 85, 115, 149; Fox Photos 72; Central Press Photos 113, 150; Periodicals Art Library 155; Camera Press 157

Introduction

Great lovers with their hot-blooded intrigues and secret passions, their lusty appetites and scorn of convention, crop up in the most unexpected places in history.

In this book you will find kings who have risked their thrones to satisfy their desires, great public figures who have thrown their reputations to the wind for just one more embrace, and writers, artists and actors whose love affairs have been more turbulent than anything they could invent.

Great lovers do not conform to a set pattern. The most devastating emotions have been roused by men who look like the average bank clerk, and women past their first bloom have attracted hapless victims like passion flowers. Love on this scale is not a tidy business. But it is fascinating to catch a glimpse of these passionate people, falling in love and out again, hurrying from bedroom to bedroom, risking everything for the sake of 'l'amour' . . .

Chapter
One

GENIUS FOR LOVE

Casanova

Casanova died in 1798 and his name passed into our language. His reputation as the greatest lover of all time, his genius in the art of seduction, gave him immortality. For a time after his death people had begun to wonder if he was not in fact a myth, a fable, a creation of the fancy.

He had, it was said, made love to hundreds of women. He had performed with distinction as a magician, scholar, gambler, spy, police agent, historian and raconteur.

Casanova himself wrote, 'The chief occupation of my life has been to cultivate the pleasures of the senses. Nothing has ever meant as much to me as that. Feeling myself born for the fair sex, I have always loved it, and have been loved in return as often as possible.'

His memoirs, discovered after his death in the Castle of Dux, where he spent the last years of his life as librarian to Count Waldstein, were so sensational that his detractors declared they were works of fiction. Within forty years three versions of *L'Histoire de ma Vie* appeared, each one more adulterated and expurgated than the last.

The restoration of Casanova to his glorious, bawdy, full-blooded self started in the 1880s and has been going on ever since.

Confirmation of his reality, for those who must have facts and figures, may be found in contemporary police archives, in dispatches from Venetian spies and ambassadors, in accounts of him by people living at the time, and in a plaque in the wall of a church at Duchcov: 'Jakob Casanova, Venedig 1725–Dux 1798'. He lies somewhere under the grass in the churchyard of St Barbara, near Dux, though the iron cross said to have been erected at the time has long gone.

Through his own words, he comes to life again in the full vigour of his manhood. Tall, swarthy, aquiline, with wide shoulders and a fine head of hair, he dominated the scene with his commanding presence. The elaborate silks and laces of his foppish dress, the heavy perfume with which he drenched himself and the powder sprinkled in his hair did nothing to conceal his enormous stamina and virility.

Given fifteen minutes, he claimed, he could seduce all but the most virtuous of women. Given time he could make his partner remember him for life. Nuns, duchesses, whores, peasants, actresses and aged crones were all gathered in. He was a lover of consummate skill and left most of his amours sighing when he could not stay longer.

Giacomo Casanova, the eldest of a family of six, was born in Venice on 2 April 1725. His father was an actor and his mother the daughter of a shoemaker. Both his parents went on the stage after his birth and his education was badly neglected. His grandmother thought he was an imbecile and took him to a sorceress, who, it was claimed, returned his faculties to him.

In his teens he was clever enough to attend the University of Padua where he took his degree in both canon and civil law. Returning to Venice, he prepared to enter the church, receiving the tonsure and minor orders from the Patriarch of Venice. An ecclesiastical career, he felt, would at least save him from marriage, a word he could never hear without feeling faint.

His first sermon was a disaster. His vision was clouded with passion for a girl called Angela, sitting in a front pew. He could not see his words and had to feign illness. He did not see the inside of a church again for two years.

The loss of his virtue, typically, was achieved with the help of not one but two attractive girls. He fell in love with two sisters at once, Nanette and Marton Savorgnan, nieces of the pious old lady who employed the luscious Angela. They sympathized with his lack of success as a priest. He was touched by their concern and suggested one evening that as a gesture of friendship they should all three undress and pass the night in the same bed. When they hesitated he seemed offended. What had they to fear? They were two to one. They undressed and joined him in bed where each in turn was wooed and overcome. The double affair lasted until he left Venice.

At eighteen Casanova set off for Southern Italy and from this time on lived largely by his wits. He was taken into the service of distinguished men, talked his way into the most brilliant society, and by means of introductions gradually moved up the social ladder. When he returned to Rome it was with a letter of introduction to Cardinal Aquaviva who financed a visit to Constantinople.

Though Constantinople had seemed romantic at a distance, Casanova was bored by the Turkish capital. He amused himself by making the acquaintance of a wealthy Turk, Yusuf Ali, who was eager to secure him as a son-in-law. Casanova, however, did not fancy either the turban or wedlock and fled to Corfu, where he spent most of his time gambling. He would stake money on any game but he became a past master at Faro, then the rage of Europe. He thought nothing of gambling all night, all day and the next night, without a break.

Learning to play Faro cost him dearly. He returned to Venice almost penniless. Playing the violin in a theatre orchestra was the best he could do for himself. He was rescued by a man who had become his protector and father figure, Signor de Bragadin, a wealthy and important member of the Venetian senate.

Casanova had been of great help to Signor Bragadin when he suffered a stroke, saving him from an unscrupulous quack. From that time on the senator treated him like an adopted son, on many occasions rescuing him from financial difficulty.

It was about this time that Casanova met Henriette, the woman for whom he kept a special place in his memory. She loved him and wrote to him till his death. He had gone to Cesana to earn some money in his capacity as a sorcerer and magician. A farmer called Caperani believed there was hidden treasure in his fields and, hearing of Casanova's reputation in the occult field, paid him a substantial fee to find it. Having completed certain rites, which included bathing the farmer's nubile daughter, the heavens opened and such a terrible thunderstorm followed he was almost converted to a belief in his own powers. He decided to leave Cesana immediately.

Next morning as he was preparing to depart from the inn where he had been staying, he heard a commotion in the passage. The local bishop, having heard that a man at the inn had been sleeping with a woman who was not his wife, had sent the police.

Casanova was enraged at such meddling interference. He helped to get rid of the law then introduced himself. The man in question turned out to be an elderly but handsome Hungarian captain. The companion by his side, hiding under a sheet, was, he declared, a French officer. When the 'officer' emerged from the bedclothes, Casanova rocked with laughter. Under a jauntily perched cap he saw a fresh, laughing face, tumbled copper curls and blue eyes belonging to the most ravishing girl he had ever seen. Her name was Henriette.

Asked to join the Hungarian captain and his mistress at breakfast, Casanova was aware that Henriette looked more stunning than ever in her tight-fitting blue army officer's uniform. He made up his mind to accompany the two of them to Parma. Soon it became obvious that she preferred Casanova to the elderly Hungarian and the transfer was made.

Young and ardent, Casanova and Henriette lived in bliss for several months, but his money began to run out. Henriette, practical above all things, abandoned their idyll and disappeared with a new and wealthy lover. Before she left, however, she slipped into Casanova's pocket five rolls of one hundred louis d'or each, a very large sum but 'feeble consolation for a heart overwhelmed by a cruel separation'.

Casanova's career progressed, though not without causing considerable envy. Many important people wanted him under lock and key. They were jealous of his supreme reputation as a lover, his gambling, his arrogance, his dabbling with sorcery. One day in July 1755, the order went out for his arrest, dead or alive. He was never charged but condemned to five years imprisonment without trial. A religious satire he had written as a youth was used as a pretext, but the report on which the tribunal acted has since been discovered. In it he is described as a disturber of the peace, a dangerous character who lived by exploiting his friends, and the possessor of forbidden works on magic and necromancy.

He was confined to the Leads, the infamous ratridden dungeons of Venice, from which, it was said, it was impossible to escape. But Casanova did escape in a remarkable and highly dangerous scramble over the roofs of Venice. Once free he hailed a gondola and was rowed off.

After this famous escapade, which proved his wit and courage, he fled to Paris where he performed a miracle of reincarnation for the gullible Marchioness d'Urfé who believed in his magic. In Paris he also satisfied his love of rich food and good wine. Food apparently aroused almost the same lust in him as did women. He would seduce his mistresses with larks and anchovies as an hors d'oeuvres and he enjoyed nothing more than sliding an oyster between the breasts of his paramour and delicately eating it *in situ*.

Casanova usually came out of his affairs unscathed but there was one encounter in Italy he was never to forget. Visiting the Duc de Matalone in Naples, he was introduced to the aristocrat's beautiful young mistress, Leonilda. He fell so desperately in love with her that he begged the duke to grant him her hand in marriage. The duke, amused to see Casanova so truly smitten, agreed. But the girl's mother had to be sent for, to put her name to the marriage contract. On the day she was expected to arrive, Casanova was forced to leave the palace on urgent business. When he returned, in time for supper, he found the duke, Leonilda and Leonilda's mother waiting for him, all in a state of happy excitement. When the latter saw Casanova, she screamed and fainted. Casanova recognized her with horror. It was one of his old loves, Anna Maria Vallati, who had given birth to his child seventeen years before. He had been about to marry his own daughter.

The year 1763 marked a turning point, the beginning of his decline. He arrived in England with relief for he had become dangerously involved in the affair of Madame d'Urfé and it was being said that he had swindled her out of a million francs. He admired the English and found no difficulty in getting invitations to all the proper social events. But he was only too aware of the loneliness of his Pall Mall apartment when he returned to it at night. He became involved with a sharp little prostitute called Marianne Charpillon who outwitted him. To his shame and humiliation she cost him 2,000 guineas and refused to grant him her favours. In revenge he bought a parrot and taught it to repeat: in French: 'Charpillon is a greater whore than her mother'.

Casanova left England in the spring of 1764, travelled for a time, and returned to Venice in 1772 after years of exile to find that his escape from the Leads had made him a folk hero. He was even invited to dinner by new members of the Tribunal who all wanted to know how he had done it. He became a secret agent for the inquisitors, but the work did not suit him; he could never keep out of trouble for long. An affair of honour, a threatened duel and bitter words drove him from his birthplace once more and for the last time.

In February 1784 he had the great good fortune to meet Count Joseph Charles de Waldstein who asked him to take charge of his library at his castle at Dux. For the next thirteen years, the last years of his life, he dutifully catalogued Count Waldstein's library of 40,000 volumes, complained about everything, suspected everyone. Only one thing really interested him – the story of his life. He relived all his past amours, his adventures, triumphs and disasters, and gave them to posterity.

Pablo Picasso

Pablo Picasso needed the love of a woman as much as he needed paint and canvas, for the great artist was both a genius and a Don Juan. Every time he fell in love he was inspired by revolutionary ideas and swept along on a tide of creativity. Both the beginning and the ending of his love affairs were reflected in his painting. The seven great loves of his life were each connected with a major period of his work.

Picasso had been born in Malaga on the south coast of Spain on 25 October 1881, the only male child of a family which could be traced back on his father's side to Old Castile at the beginning of the 16th century. His mother, a dark, petite woman, who passed on her looks to her adored son, came from a once famous family of goldsmiths in Majorca. From his earliest days the only thing that really interested Picasso was drawing and painting. The portraits he painted at the age of ten were astonishing. Their technique was said to be that of an already established artist. Fortunately his family recognized the incredible driving force in him. His father, Don José, a sad, disillusioned, failed artist, sensing the genius in his son helped and guided him all the way.

The family moved to Barcelona when Pablo was a youth. It was a place bursting with intellectual life and he discovered there the existence of the avant garde movements in Europe. He also discovered his vigorous sexual appetite. He studied in Barcelona and Madrid but knew all along that one day he would have to go to Paris. His first visit was in 1900. He felt lost, awkward, out of place and could speak very little French. It was not until four years later, after several visits, that he felt ready to become part of that colourful, impoverished world that centred on Montmartre.

He moved into a studio in the 'Bateau Lavoir', a ramshackle, almost derelict row of apartments in the rue Ravignan. It was a building which had neither gas nor electricity; it let in the wind in winter and heated up like an oven in summer. There was only one cold water tap to serve the whole building and it was there he often met a fellow painter, a student at the Ecole des Beaux Arts. Her name was Fernande Olivier, and she was an extraordinarily beautiful young woman.

One stormy evening Fernande rushed into the Bateau Lavoir dripping wet and bumped into Picasso in the corridor. He was carrying a tiny kitten in his arms. They laughed about the rain and Picasso smiled at her with his enigmatic black eyes and offered her the kitten. He invited her to his studio where he offered her a cup of hot coffee. Before the night was out she was his mistress.

Both of them were experiencing their first genuine passion after many casual experiences. Fernande had posed for several painters and sculptors in Paris, including Dufy, and had become more than a model to some of them. With Picasso she knew instinctively things would be different. At this period of his life he was short and stocky with a face the colour of parchment, magnetic black eyes and a lock of black hair falling over his forehead. He dressed like a workman in blue cotton trousers and jacket but there was something of the aristocrat about him and his features expressed terrific willpower and strength. There was usually a poppy-coloured belt around his hips or a scarlet scarf around his neck for he styled himself as a bit of a dandy.

Fernande moved in with him. They were desperately poor but their poverty did not worry her. She was a passive sensual creature who spent hours lying on a divan reading newspapers and smoking cigarettes in an amber holder. Picasso did many of the household chores, including the shopping. Like a true Spaniard, he was intensely jealous and did not want her to meet other men unless he was with her.

Their apartment could almost be described as squalid. Everything was worn out and shabby, the floor strewn with cigarette ends and squashed tubes of paint. It consisted of a tiny hall, a bedroom almost entirely taken up by a divan and a large studio in which the paint was peeling off the walls and the window panes were tinted blue to reduce glare. It was difficult to move around because of the unbelievable quantity of junk that Picasso had picked up in the flea markets. He was a compulsive collector of bric-à-brac all his life and never threw anything away.

On summer days when the temperature inside became torrid, Picasso would paint with his studio door thrown wide open on to the corridor where other tenants could see him working at his easel, stark naked except for a scarf tied round his loins. He was very proud of his strong, muscular shoulders and his delicate wrists and ankles and enjoyed lingering, appreciative glances from the opposite sex. On bitter, winter days, when it became unbearably cold, Picasso and Fernande would huddle together in bed for warmth.

They were so poor that once when Picasso had been given a commission to paint a still life of flowers he had to do it without using white because he could not afford a fresh tube of paint. During his affair with Fernande he painted some of the great pictures of his 'blue period' and though his output was prodigious, he only got a few francs apiece for pictures he sold.

He cleared out a lumber room adjoining the studio and turned it into a sort of shrine for his love. On a packing case draped with a red silk cloth he arranged the souvenirs of their life together: a dark red paper rose, a couple of cheap vases won at a fair, a pair of Fernande's earrings, the blouse she had been wearing the night of the storm.

Though life was hard they could be heard laughing and singing together and the communal life they shared with other artists softened the harshness of poverty.

Most of the time through this period Picasso was making beautiful drawings and pictures of circus figures: acrobats, tumblers, harlequins and clowns. One day the art dealer Ambroise Vollard came to see him in the rue Ravignan. He spent ages thoughtfully sorting through canvasses then, to Picasso's joy, bought thirty paintings for which he paid 2,000 francs. News spread like wildfire through the art world that Picasso had been taken up by Vollard and his friends began to call him 'maître'.

Connection with Vollard meant security. In the autumn of 1909 Picasso moved an ecstatic Fernande to a comfortable apartment in the boulevard Clichy where they had hot running water out of the taps and electricity. A new Fernande emerged. Now that Picasso was earning real money she developed a passion for dresses, hats and furs. Once she spent all their housekeeping money on perfume. She also decided that a resident maid was essential. After a time there were quarrels, sulks and reconciliations until Picasso began to think nostalgically of their old days together in the rue Ravignan. It was after one particularly fierce quarrel and passionate reconciliation that he painted his first truly cubist picture.

In the summer of 1912 he was introduced to a friend of Fernande's called Marcelle Humbert, a woman whose refined elegance and delicate beauty completely captivated him. It was love at first sight. Only after a time did Fernande realize that Picasso was being unfaithful to her. She had to do something. Herself in the throes of an infatuation with Italian painter Ubaldo Oppi, she hoped to make Picasso jealous by running away with him. Her action had the opposite effect to what she intended. Picasso, finding himself free, packed his bags and went off to Ceret, taking Marcelle with him. The little town, idyllic in the full beauty of Spring, was spoiled when many of their Bohemian friends followed them, to find out how Picasso's affair was progressing.

Pablo Picasso

THE WORLD'S GREATEST LOVERS

Eventually Fernande herself arrived, full of remorse and despair. But it was too late. Picasso told his friend Gertrude Stein, the writer: 'I am still spellbound by her beauty but I can't stand her caprices any more.' To bring their relationship to a definite end he left with Marcelle for Avignon. Years later, when he heard Fernande was ill he sent her a million francs to get proper medical treatment. But they were never to meet again. After she died alone in her apartment in 1966, a little heart-shaped mirror that Picasso had once given her was found in a jewel box.

Picasso and Marcelle rented a house in the village of Sorgnes near Avignon. He had a burst of creative energy to celebrate the beginning of his new love. He called Marcelle Eva because she was the 'first woman' in his life and though he could not paint a realistic portrait of her because he was in the middle of experimenting with cubism he paid homage to her by inscribing two of the pictures he painted in 1912 'J'aime Eva'. She appeared as a figure in some of his works and a picture bearing the inscription 'Ma Jolie' was found on the kitchen wall of their apartment. When Picasso left, Khanweiler, the cubist art dealer, sent a team of experts from Paris to remove the painting from the wall.

After Provence the lovers settled into a well-appointed studio in Montparnasse, but their happiness was to be short-lived. Marcelle began to be racked by fits of coughing. The doctor diagnosed TB and she died at the beginning of 1916. Picasso was grief-stricken by the loss of his graceful, delicate partner and too miserable to work. It was altogether a sad year for him. His father died, too, and as a pacifist he found himself terribly alone and isolated as most of his friends had volunteered to serve in the war then raging over Europe.

He would eat alone at the Café Rotonde in Montparnasse and walk the streets rather than go back to the apartment where he had lived with Marcelle. He moved house again, renting a small suburban villa with an overgrown garden in the rue Victor Hugo in Montrouge. Soon he began to feel the place was ill-fated. It was burgled, flooded and cursed with a chilly atmosphere. Though he took women back there for casual affairs, they meant nothing to him and made him even unhappier.

Jean Cocteau rescued him from this gloom. He asked Picasso if he would design sets and costumes for the controversial, ultra-modern work *Parade* which was to be staged by the great Diaghilev for the Russian Ballet. Picasso had never worked for the theatre before but he went with Cocteau to Rome where rehearsals were in progress and soon became excited by the ideas which poured from his ever fertile mind.

At one rehearsal he met Olga Koklova, a dancer with the Russian Ballet. She was the daughter of an officer in the Russian Artillery. Her supple grace, sleek dark hair and almost childlike simplicity intrigued Picasso. In a company with extremely lax morals she displayed a flower-like innocence. He was tired of easy conquests and longed for an intense relationship again. Olga was receptive to his wooing. She was weary of the vagabond life she had to lead with the Ballet and ready to settle down. Picasso seemed to offer her stability and a position in cultured society. Her failure to realize that he was a free spirit and true Bohemian was the root of a great deal of future trouble.

For the moment, however, there was not a cloud on the horizon. Picasso painted Olga in a white mantilla and sent the portrait home to his mother. Then, to show how serious he was, he took his intended bride to Barcelona and introduced her to his family. Picasso's mother made her welcome but, detecting her bourgeois nature, tried to warn her by saying 'I don't think any woman can be happy with him and his way of life.'

They were married on 12 July 1918 with Cocteau, Diaghilev and the poet Apollinaire as witnesses. Picasso gave himself up to the infinite pleasure of educating his young wife in the ways of love. To please her, he even tried to turn himself into a society artist, dedicated to receptions, elegant dinners and entertaining. He also took a handsome apartment near the Champs Elysées and was quite amused at first by the social strata into which marriage drew him.

As usual his new love brought a new phase of creativity. He amazed the world by his explosion of artistic genius. Still painting for the ballet, he also produced superb still-life pictures and other canvasses of startling originality. They were happy years. His son Paolo was born in 1921 and he painted exquisite, tender portraits of this adored child.

But slowly, over the years, the naïve sprite of the Russian ballet turned into a bourgois with the stiff, formal outlook of her kind. Their apartment was handsome, but it was not the home of an artist. Frustrated by the houseproud Olga, Picasso rented an apartment above their own and kept it as his own domain, a place where he could paint, drop his cigarette ends and collect his incredible junk. By 1924, under the influence of the surrealist movement, he began to paint deformed portraits in which people had several heads, dismembered legs and eyes and noses in the strangest places. In the future, whenever he faced an emotional crisis he reverted to this style.

Their life together became stormy. Olga would not adapt herself to Picasso's Bohemian habits and did not understand him. He was tired of trying to conform to her way of life. Her scenes of rage, anger and jealousy made him utterly dismayed but for a long time he tried to placate her for fear of losing his son should they separate.

One day in 1931, walking in Paris near the Galeries Lafayette, he bumped into a tall, fresh-faced blonde with the bronzed, athletic look of a northern goddess. They fell into conversation and he learned she was Swiss, 17 years old and her name was Marie Thérèse Walter. Her life was devoted to sport, but she had such a gay, gentle, undemanding personality that Picasso fell in love with her. After the Slavic intensity of his wife she was like a cool, refreshing stream.

Marie Thérèse loved Picasso simply and deeply and did not want any part of his fame. They did not live together very much and he did not introduce her to his friends, but for years she remained a gay, gentle influence in the background. She had a softening influence on his work. The monsters disappeared and he began to paint full, harmonious figures which glorified the female body. Marie Thérèse is seen in the famous 'Femme au Fauteuil', and again in his large sculptures.

In 1935 Picasso left Olga for good. He found it difficult to discuss separation with her. After all she had been part of his life for seventeen years. A divorce suit was begun but the decree was never made absolute. A happier event that year was the birth of his daughter Maria at Boisgeloup, the beautiful country house Picasso retreated to with Marie Thérèse in an effort to escape from the still hovering Olga. He would not be free of his first wife for many years. She would follow him to exhibitions, screaming abuse at any woman in his company, hang around the places he often frequented, even appear threateningly on beaches when he swam in the sea.

During this time, however, he found yet another companion who was to live with him in the ten difficult years ahead. He threw himself into the new affair in the autumn of 1935 when he already had two women competing for his attentions. His meeting with Dora Maar was over a bowl of ripe cherries at the famous cafe, Deux Magots. He was fascinated by the young woman's sensitive face, lit up by the palest blue eyes and tried to think of ways to get to know her better. She solved the problem for him. She was a photographer, a close friend of great camera artists like Man Ray and André Breton, and she often worked as a freelance journalist. This gave her an excuse to call on Picasso. Commissioned to do a feature article about him, she asked to take photographs in his apartment . . . the affair began.

His love life at this stage has certain elements of farce. He now had two mistresses to keep happy, knowing that Olga could be waiting round any corner, ready to leap out and scream at him. His Swiss love contented him with her sunny temperament and beautiful body but he turned to Dora for the fresh stimulus he needed in order to paint. The two women hated each other. Picasso enjoyed their rivalry and wickedly took pains to provoke their jealousy. One day they flew at each other in his presence and he did nothing to stop the fight.

He rented an enormous loft studio in the rue des Grand Augustins. Dora proved an excellent companion as well as a passionate lover. She fascinated and excited him and inspired the most dramatic period of his life which saw his work rise to tragic heights of greatness.

Two terrible events which were to influence his work were the Spanish Civil War, which broke out in 1936, and the tide of Fascism leading to the Second

World War. Throughout the Spanish war he gave financial support and sold pictures from his private collection to help refugees and children's organizations. On the morning of 28 April Nazi planes helping the Spanish fascists bombed the little Basque town of Guernica. The casualties were horrifying. Sick with anger and grief, Picasso recorded 'Guernica' for all time in one of the greatest works of its kind ever produced.

When war broke out in Europe he shut himself away. He watched the Germans march into Paris from his studio window. 'They are another race', he said sadly. The few painters in German uniform he met were not turned away. He talked with them, showed them his work and presented them with postcards of 'Guernica'. He knew Hitler had designated him as a degenerate artist but he was determined to see the war through in Paris with Dora.

During the four years of the occupation he hardly left his studio, holding court there for those who wished to see him. He had tried to cling to his love for Dora but she had a changeable character, which made her subject to fits of depression and sudden rages which ended in tears. Before the war ended another woman entered his life.

He was now in his early 60s but magnificently preserved, his body strong and muscular, his face lean and commanding. When they met in May 1943 Françoise Gilot was only 21, a young painter whose beauty and talent enchanted him. She was graceful and tall, with a slender waist, corn-coloured hair and emerald-green eyes.

Françoise did not capitulate immediately. She played the coquette, sometimes displaying ardour, sometimes indifference. He soon found he was unable to hide his passion, but was determined not to be outwitted by this young woman. He would try to shock her in public, suddenly kissing her on the mouth or fondling her breasts in front of their friends. Once he asked her to take off her clothes and lie down beside him only to gaze at her with a cool, professional eye then tell her to get dressed again. She describes their 'prolonged fencing match' in the book she wrote about their love affair. It went on for three years until May 1946 when Françoise gave in, left her grandmother's house and went to live with Picasso on the Côte d'Azur.

When Dora realized what was going on there were terrible scenes. She became subject to hallucinations and a religious fanatic. Picasso took her to a clinic for the best treatment he could afford but she was lost to her dreams and spiritual visions. Their last meeting was painful. She hurled accusations at him when he insensitively suggested that Dora tell Françoise face to face that it was all over between them.

In the south of France Picasso regained his youth, became bronzed and agile, swimming and sunbathing with his beautiful Françoise. He painted the most marvellous pictures of the female body and also found a new inspiration in ceramics. Working in the little town of Vallauris, completely absorbed in the new medium, he turned out 2,000 pieces in 18 months. Vallauris was suddenly famous. Picasso was made an honorary citizen and they celebrated his birthday each year.

At the end of 1948 he settled down close to Vallauris in a house called 'La Galloise', set in the midst of orange groves. Françoise complained that it was too small and cramped and they had little privacy there, for Picasso was now an international figure and hundreds beat a path to his door. Françoise was also annoyed by the fact that the townspeople, knowing she was not his wife, called her 'La Picasette', meaning Picasso's girl. She did not intend to be laughed at or to play second fiddle to his greatness. Gradually quarrels and disagreements spoiled their life together. Picasso felt Françoise should have children to fulfil herself and persuaded her to become the mother of his children, His son, Claude, was born in 1947 and his daughter Paloma, in 1949. He was delighted with them but Françoise, still not satisfied, became assertive. He began painting her in grotesque twisted postures. To cap it all Olga turned up as he bathed in the sea, shrieking at him from the beach that he was still her husband in the eyes of the Spanish law.

Picasso's friends had been expecting something drastic to happen for some time. He had been seeing other women and generally flaunting his amazing fitness and virility. On 30 September 1953 Françoise left with the children and returned to Paris to begin a new life.

There was a bullring in Vallauris and Picasso was able to go to the *toros* again as he had with his father when he was a small boy in Malaga. People noticed that more and more often he was accompanied by a petite brunette with brilliant blue eyes. Her name was Jacqueline Roque and she was a young divorcée with a six-year-old daughter. Picasso began to paint her, a sure proof of his deep interest. He dressed her in Turkish costume, in Provençal dress and as a Spanish woman with a mantilla, but the most famous portrait shows her as 'Madam Z', revealing her natural Mediterranean warmth.

Jacqueline was to be his last love. She was gentle, devoted, adoring and was content to sit for hours watching him work. Moreover she was a good housekeeper and provided him with a comfortable home, well run, with meals on time. She also helped him organise his business life. She dealt with banks, lawyers, dealers and publishers, answered his letters and kept a catalogue of his works.

At 74 he was more vigorous than ever and gaily moved into an extraordinary villa called 'Le Californie', a folly built by a champagne merchant in the hills above Cannes. Not content with that he also took on the imposing Château de Vauvenarges, an old fortress with four turrets and a fine gateway. He finally settled down at a house in Mougins, built on a hill overlooking the village. His

Picasso and Jacqueline Roque arriving at the Cannes Film Festival

life from then on was confined mostly to his new home, though he would swim occasionally at Golfe Juan or visit a familiar restaurant. His work continued in a steady stream and on his 80 birthday he did a flamenco dance on a table while his friends cheered and clapped.

He married Jacqueline and she was to be the last of his numerous loves. Or almost the last. He had always regarded death as a woman and he knew that lady was waiting for him.

Lord Byron

Were Byron and his half-sister, Augusta Leigh, lovers? The question has haunted generations of those intrigued by the romantic poet with the reputation of being 'mad, bad and dangerous to know'.

George Gordon, sixth Lord Byron, born on 22 January 1788, was the son of a handsome rake known to his family as 'mad Jack'. This same black sheep was also the father of Augusta. Byron's mother was a Scottish heiress called Catherine of Gight, a Celt with such a bad temper she once bit a piece out of a saucer. Augusta's mother was the wife of Lord Carmarthen who caused a major scandal by eloping with rakish Jack and marrying him after her divorce.

Brother and sister met for the first time in 1802 when Byron was fourteen and Augusta, nineteen. To the boy who suffered bitterly from awareness of his club foot and a tendency to stoutness, she seemed like an angel of understanding. Gentle, sensual, dark, with a beautiful curved mouth, she fitted exactly Byron's idea of a perfect woman. But of course she was forbidden fruit. She was also engaged to their cousin, George Leigh. 'Can't you drive this cousin of ours out of your pretty little head?' he begged her. But she went through with her plans, married the horsey Colonel Leigh and settled down to be a country wife in Newmarket.

As the years went by, however, and Byron grew to be one of the most handsome and fascinating men of his day, the two found themselves drawn to each other and their affection developed into an intense passion. Byron called her 'the one whom I most loved' and even confessed to his bride on their wedding night that no woman would ever possess as much of his love as his sister Augusta.

Byron had a miserable childhood and spent most of his life making up for it by indulging his passionate, sensual nature. When he was a boy his mother's moods of depression alternated with bursts of tenderness or furious temper. She once called him a 'lame brat' and the words seared his soul. He had a thoroughly Scottish upbringing in Aberdeen and was looked after by a Calvinistic nanny who taught him that all people were sinners, predestined to damnation, a harsh doctrine that also left its mark.

When he was ten his great-uncle, always called 'the wicked Lord Byron' because he lived as a recluse with a servant girl he had named 'Lady Betty', died and left him heir to the title. He also left him Newstead Abbey, a magnificent Gothic ruin of a place in Nottinghamshire with a sinister lake and a ghost. Byron loved it. His mother took him to live there and provided him with a pretty young

nurse who added spice to her affairs ...
into bed with the young Lord. 'My p..
later. Too early, thought his mother, wh...
to school.

Byron's first real love was his cousin, M...
Hall, only a few fields away from Newstead. S...
him to the quick by saying in his hearing 'Do yo...
that lame boy!' He said the remark stayed in his h... ...nd it
certainly explained a lot of his ruthless behaviour to ... ..e. When
she married he missed a whole term at Harrow bcau... ...eartbroken.
He wrote lines to her which began 'Well, thou art hap.. ...nd it was years
before he completely got over her.

He went from Harrow to Cambridge and threw himself wholeheartedly into
the business of becoming a young rake. His mother was worried to death by his
extravagance and his drinking. 'Ruined! At 18. Great God!' she exclaimed. But
Byron had started to write poetry and that gradually became as important to
him as other pleasures. Then, still inclined to stoutness, he began to follow a
strict regime which he summarized as follows: 'Much physic, much hot bathing
and much violent exercise.'

He emerged from this self-inflicted torture ready to make half the women in
Britain swoon, giving the name 'Byronic' to a certain kind of male beauty. His
figure was now slim and elegant. Dark curls clustered round his head, his grey
eyes were fringed with long, dark lashes; his well-shaped mouth, cleft chin and
smooth, pale brow combined to give his face a look of classic nobility.

At Cambridge, however, he had gained a reputation as a profligate and
gambler and now he plunged headfirst into London life. 'I am buried in an abyss
of sensuality', he informed his great and brilliant friend, John Cam Hobhouse,
later to be Lord Brougham. But it is important to remember that Byron always
liked to exaggerate his wickedness for dramatic effect.

His unfulfilled love for Mary Chaworth lingered on and he had failed to
persuade his sister Augusta not to marry, so in 1809 he decided to travel in
Europe and the Near East and forget them both. After a farewell party at
Newstead Abbey he sailed from Falmouth with Hobhouse and did not return to
England for two years.

Byron cut his teeth on various love affairs abroad, then once back in London
decided to give himself up to his poetry. He only half-succeeded. His club foot,
which he did his best to conceal, proved no obstacle to his success with the
opposite sex. Women gazed instead at that pale face with its arrogantly sensual
lines and were lost. Suddenly, he woke up one morning to find himself famous.
On 10 March 1812 the first two Cantos of *Childe Harold* were published. The epic
was greeted with near hysteria and sold like hot cakes. Some people tried to

Lord Byron

identify Byron with his hero and were convinced that he had a hidden life. Mounds of invitations arrived at his lodgings in St James's Street. It was said you could not sit down at a dinner table in London without hearing the constant repetition of his name.

Of course what most fascinated women was the hint of scandal about him. Behind the pale beauty many suspected darkness and mystery. He revelled in the notoriety, and no doubt derived much satisfaction from it. He had a keen sense of humour and satirical wit which permeated a great deal of his work.

One woman who literally threw herself at him was the wild, delicate hoyden Lady Caroline Lamb, daughter of the Earl of Bessborough. At her first meeting with Byron she turned on her heel saying that the very sight of that handsome face made her feel faint. They were introduced again at Lady Holland's and he was entranced by her huge brown eyes, short, tumbled curls and boyish figure. Her tantalizing first rejection of him, then the experience of meeting the pretty creature face to face, was a challenge Byron could not resist.

For a few months he was in love with her then, just as suddenly, cooled off. The wild extravagance of her passion had proved too much for him. He had awakened her sexually. 'The tumult, the ardour, the romance bewildered my reason,' she wrote after one lovers' meeting. She besieged him with her emotions and when they quarrelled tried to stab herself, first with a knife, then with a piece of broken glass. She exposed him to public ridicule and that he could not forgive. At the beginning of their affair he was telling her that her heart was a little volcano – 'It pours lava through your veins and yet I cannot wish it a bit colder' – and he assured her, 'I have always thought you the cleverest, most agreeable, absurd, amiable, perplexing, dangerous fascinating little being.' Before long, however, he was moaning, 'this dream, this delirium . . . it must pass away'. She sent him some of her pubic hair, asking for his in return. Her immodesty put him off even more.

When Lady Caroline's mother tried to persuade her to go to Ireland, hoping that with the sea between them the affair would come to an end, Caro asked Byron to elope with her. He took her back to Lady Bessborough as though she were a naughty child and in the end she had to settle for Ireland. From there she bombarded him with letters.

Byron did the only thing possible to stop Caroline pestering him. He took a new mistress, the Countess of Oxford, a beautiful bluestocking who believed in free love and was twice his age. He declared that the autumn of her beauty was preferable to another woman's springtime and when Caro wrote asking for confirmation of his love he replied: 'Lady Caro, our affections are not our own . . . mine are engaged. I love another. I am no longer your lover.'

In the midst of all this he met Annabella Milbanke. She, too, was a bluestocking, a clever, intellectual girl who specialized in mathematics, theology and Greek. She was only 20 but liked life to be orderly and systematic. Byron's friends tried to make him see that they were not even remotely suited, but he was in raptures about her 'nutbrown looks' and had no doubt added to the list of her charms the fact that she was an heiress. Annabella was quite bowled over by his famous looks, came to the conclusion that he needed saving from himself, and she would do the saving. He called her 'my princess of the parallelograms' and proposed. To his amazement, she refused him.

Suddenly Byron's half-sister, Augusta, arrived on the London scene. They had been writing to each other for years, a charming, lively correspondence that showed their affection. But in the hot summer of 1813 Augusta was bored, restless and dissatisfied. Living at Newmarket with her three daughters, she hardly ever saw her husband other than when he appeared for the races. She packed her bags and descended on Byron and he was reminded once again that his sister, with her dark, sensual grace, was his ideal woman.

Byron's whole life had been devoted to satisfying his sensations. Now, it is almost certain, he gave away to his desires once again and discovered the sensation of forbidden love. In her biography of the poet, Lady Elizabeth Longford says, 'Gradually, however, there was another sensation not so pleasant as the first – sexual guilt. Ill-treated by her husband, Augusta would do anything Byron wanted. It is as certain as these things can be that she was his lover. Her unthinking acquiescence in his crime must have increased his guilty torment.'

Augusta constantly dominated his thoughts and feelings. At last he could no longer bear the burden without telling someone else. Lady Melbourne seemed the ideal person. She had been acting as go-between for him with Annabella, but was a modern thinker and feminist. Byron told her how this love for his sister made all other loves seem insipid. Their intentions, he admitted, had been very different and when they failed to adhere to them it had been due to her 'weakness' and his 'folly'. Lady Melbourne was appalled and told him so. Byron had some wild idea about going abroad and taking Augusta with him. Lady Melbourne implored him to go abroad by all means, but to leave Augusta behind.

When Byron celebrated his 26th birthday Augusta was heavily pregnant. For the moment only Lady Melbourne knew of his feelings and she dreaded to think what society would say if the 'truth' came out. The press had already described Lord Byron as 'a deformed Richard III, an atheist rebel and a devil'. What would they do if they found out about his relations with his sister?

Augusta gave birth to a daughter. Could he be the father? Byron himself, apparently, had doubts and he was never as fond of this child, christened Medora, as he was of Augusta's other children who were undoubtedly fathered by Colonel Leigh.

Lady Caroline Lamb

Ten months had gone by since he last saw Annabella Milbanke, proposed to her, and received her refusal. He decided he must try to lay the ghosts of past love affairs and commit himself to a decent marriage. Various candidates were put forward by well-meaning friends but he would not consider them. He became involved with the pedantic young bluestocking again and they drifted into a marriage which both were to regret bitterly.

Though he could be a sparkling and charming companion, he behaved abominably on the honeymoon, taunting Annabella with his love for Augusta and hinting that the child she had just given birth to was his.

Marriage was not as bad as he had expected. They had some pleasant times together at the Milbanke home at Seaham in the north of England, but Byron began to feel cut off, trapped, and insisted they move back to London. They collected Augusta on the way and Annabella, seeing brother and sister together, had her worst suspicions confirmed. Byron, torn apart by his conflicting emotions, behaved even worse than on his honeymoon. 'There were times,' Annabella wrote later, 'when I could have plunged a dagger into his heart.' Strangely enough his behaviour drew the two women together and Annabella began to have hopes that she could 'save' them both. 'His misfortune is an habitual passion for excitement,' she told Augusta.

When their daughter Ada was born Annabella began to suspect that debts, drunkenness and remorse over Augusta had driven Byron mad. He told her they could no longer afford to live in style in London and she was to go home to her parents at their estate in Leicestershire. They said goodbye for the last time on 14 January 1815. She could take no more and had come to the conclusion that she had fallen in love with Lucifer himself. The truth was, they were ill-matched from the start.

Byron himself seemed to accept her judgement, saying bitterly in one letter to her, 'It is my destiny to ruin all I come near.' Annabella eventually admitted to a confidante that her secret reason for parting with Byron was her growing suspicion of his incest. Augusta was pregnant again and this time people were giving voice to their suspicions. She could no longer stay for even short visits at Byron's house in Piccadilly. She went off to resume her duties as a woman of the bedchamber to Queen Charlotte, who would not have believed in such goings on, even if she had been told about them.

The separation of Byron and Annabella caused no little scandal. Female society turned against the poet, though women still peeped from behind their fans, around doors and lace curtains to catch a glimpse of him, and their hearts beat faster at a glance from those cool grey eyes.

It was under these circumstances that Byron boarded a packet for Ostend on 25 April 1816 and left England, never to return alive. He and Augusta said goodbye to one another wretchedly and in tears. They were never to meet again. He wrote her the exquisite lines beginning:

'Thou wert the solitary star
Which rose and set not to the last . . .

His friend Hobhouse listened to him curse the hypocrisy and repressiveness of

English morality, which was driving him away and noticed that some inquisitive society women, disguising themselves as servant girls, had gathered on the quay to have one last look at the demon lover.

Byron travelled through Belgium and Switzerland in his dark green Napoleonic coach to join his friend, the poet Shelley, and his wife Mary at their hotel on the outskirts of Geneva. Also waiting for him was a hot-headed girl he hoped he had left behind in England.

At the eleventh hour before his departure Byron had become involved with 17-year-old Claire Clairmont, Mary Shelley's step-sister. She was an incurable romantic, jealous of Mary's elopement with Shelley and determined to catch herself a poet. She wrote to Byron, asking for a meeting and making it clear she was ready to be his mistress. The meeting took place somewhere in London during his last week in England. Byron had no intention of seeing her again but had unwisely given her the address in Geneva where she could write. She packed and hurried to Switzerland ahead of him.

Now the party was a foursome. He took the Villa Diodati on the Belle Rive of Lake Geneva while the Shelleys occupied a villa on the hillside above. He spoke of Claire as 'a foolish girl' but she was close to him for a brief spell and gave birth to his daughter.

Switzerland was a watershed in Byron's life. Stimulated by the company of the younger poet and by the drama of the mountains and lakes, he wrote his great poem *The Prisoner of Chillon*. When it was translated into German Byron was taken up by Goethe and his fame began to spread throughout Europe. He also climbed the Alps with Hobhouse and wrote the first two acts of his poetic drama *Manfred*.

For a time it was an idyllic life but Byron eventually made a move to end it for he did not want to be tied to Claire. He persuaded the Shelleys to take her home. He still encountered upper class English tourists in Geneva who stared at him 'as though a devil had come among them'. He wanted to get even further away from his homeland. Italy had a very strong appeal for him. He headed for Venice and the sun.

It did not take him long to find comfortable lodgings over a prosperous baker's shop. The great attraction of these premises was the baker's wife, Marianna Segati, with whom he fell 'in fathomless love'. Her husband saw no harm in her taking this English Lord as her lover, in fact he bragged about it. Marianna was a seductive, hot-blooded creature with large, liquid eyes, dark, glossy hair and the grace of a gazelle. She also had a fearful temper which she displayed when she thought her sister-in-law was trying to take her place in Byron's bed.

Rumours of her violent love for the poet travelled all over Venice and, naturally, shocked the resident English. Apart from the affair with Marianna his

Margherita Cogni

first few months in the city were comparatively respectable. He was entranced by its ancient narrow streets and canals and loved the Italian working people and shopkeepers whom he found natural, vivid and warmhearted. It was after he installed himself in the Palazzo Mocenigo overlooking the Grande Canale that he gave way to the excesses that impaired his health. The Venice Carnival, with its unspeakably dissolute entertainments, held him captive. Yet it was at this time that he wrote some of his finest poetry including the first Canto of *Don Juan* and *Manfred*, which contained some of his most profound thoughts about man's destiny.

La Segati was followed by baker's wife Margherita Cogni. He met her one day while he was out riding and was immediately drawn to the magnificent, 22-

year-old peasant, tall, strong, wild and beautiful. To keep her near him he employed her as housekeeper at his summer villa at La Mira on the river Brenta, seven miles from Venice. She, too, had a terrible temper and it was said she once took advantage of Byron's lameness and beat him in a fit of jealousy. Certainly after a few months he had had enough of her, but she refused to leave. When he finally managed to dismiss her, she threw herself into the canal from which she was rescued just in time.

This was the most dissolute period of his life. When he celebrated his 30th birthday in 1818 he was beginning to show some of the effects of his self-indulgence. He was said to have founded a harem which cost him £3,000. He boasted that it accommodated 200 women of every nationality, but he was probably exaggerating. He had become, in his biographer Lady Longford's words, 'a puffy Romeo, both comical and sad'. Yet his poetry flooded out to a disapproving world that could not help but recognize his genius, and in his debauchery he wrote one of the most beautiful lyrics in the language:

'So we'll go no more a-roving
So late into the night,
Though the heart be still as loving,
And the moon be still as bright.

For the sword outwears its sheath,
And the soul wears out the breast,
And the heart must pause to breathe,
And love itself have rest.'

At a reception held by the Countess Benzoni the 30-year-old Byron came face to face with the last love of his life. Nineteen-year-old Countess Teresa Guiccioli had been married for just three days when they met. Her husband was an elderly, eccentric landowner and the marriage had been one entirely of convenience. Byron was attracted by this striking Italian girl with golden hair, blue eyes, a fine complexion and magnificent bust and shoulders, but did not at the time foresee what the depths of his feelings for her would be. They discussed Dante together, rode on horseback under the great umbrella pines, strolled through scented gardens on balmy evenings. Soon he was writing to her, 'You have been mine and whatever is the outcome, I am and eternally shall be yours . . .' She called him 'mio Byron' in public, which was guaranteed to shock.

The Guicciolis moved to their palazzo in Ravenna and Byron was invited to rent the upper floor. He was not entirely happy about it, suspecting that the old man intended to spy on them. Nevertheless he moved in, bringing with him ten horses, for which he had been promised stabling, eight enormous dogs, three monkeys, five cats, an eagle, a crow and a falcon. After a few months he added five peacocks, two guinea hens and a crane.

Byron and his countess lived in a romantic trance. This time he was really in love. She brought such beauty and intelligence into his life that he was haunted by regrets that they had not met sooner. He quite clearly saw himself as an ageing Don Juan.

Count Guiccioli was well aware of his wife's affair with Byron but waited until he caught them together on a sofa one day before reading the riot act. He demanded she should give him up. Her answer was to ask the Pope for a separation. This was eventually granted to her and she went to live under her father's roof at the nearby Palazzo Gamba. Byron was left with her eccentric husband, the poet comically protesting that he could not possibly move out because of his vast menagerie!

Revolution was in the air and politics were soon to change all their lives. Teresa's family was well known for its sympathy with the oppressed poor. In 1821, after a fracas in which the commander of the papal troops was killed in the street in Ravenna, the Gambas, including Teresa, had to fly from the Pope's domain. Teresa left Byron in floods of tears, wondering if she would ever see him again.

Three months elapsed before he could follow. Shelley had visited him in Ravenna, finding him popular with the people there who knew he sympathized with their struggles. Byron told his friend that he was 'reformed, as far as gallantry goes'.

In October of that year Byron's travelworn Napoleonic coach rumbled out of Ravenna for the last time. He found a suitable house on the river Arno, near Pisa, only two or three minutes from where Teresa had settled with her family. They formed a new social circle, entertaining in style and giving dinners at which a mellowed Byron played host with wit and irony until the early hours of the morning. Perhaps it was just a shade too domestic, too cosy. When Lady Blessington visited him he told her, 'there is something in the poetical temperament that precludes happiness, not only to the person who has it, but to those connected with him'. To her he confessed his extraordinary presentiment that he would die in Greece.

Greece had been on his mind for some time. He was totally in sympathy with those who suffered oppression of any kind. By the beginning of April 1823 he was afire to help the struggling Greek patriots in their war of independence against the Turks. He did not dare tell Teresa that he was going to war, partly because he feared she would try to stop him. But the young countess knew well enough what was happening and she too had a presentiment that he would not return. Their last hours together almost broke her heart.

Byron was only 35 when he sailed from Genoa to Greece in July 1823 but his constitution was wrecked and his life force spent. When he landed on the beach at Missolonghi, resplendent in scarlet uniform, the Greeks hailed him as a delivering angel. But the enterprise to which Byron was committed was badly planned and ill-conceived. Missolonghi was set on a lagoon rich in malaria. Once the winter rains began the place became a disease-ridden mudbowl. His health weakened by the conditions, Byron had no strength left to fight the rheumatic fever that struck him in the spring following that appalling winter. The end came swiftly on Easter Monday, 19 April 1824 when he fell into a deep sleep after delirium. There were memorial services in every important town in Greece. In England, those who had considered him to be a demon lover, Lucifer incarnate, flocked into the streets as the cortège carrying his body made its way home for burial.

Chapter
Two

POWERFUL
PASSIONS

Palmerston

Most people remember Lord Palmerston as the Victorian prime minister who was prepared to send gunboats to the aid of beleaguered Britons. It was said that as long as a man had Palmerston and the British navy behind him he was safe anywhere.

But Palmerston had another reputation for which he was equally famous. *The Times* called him 'Lord Cupid' because of his amorous activities. Queen Victoria got very cross when he tried to seduce one of her ladies-in-waiting, and at the ripe old age of 79 he was cited as co-respondent in a famous divorce case.

His rakish reputation was combined with a brilliant career in which he became foreign secretary three times and prime minister, twice. As a politician he changed as the world around him changed. From being a diehard Tory brought up to believe that poverty and suffering were the Godgiven lot of the lower classes, he became a staunch supporter of the working man, a fierce opponent of slavery and one of the founders of the modern Liberal party. But as 'Lord Cupid' his love of pretty women, discreet seductions and dangerous flirtations never changed.

Henry John Temple, third Viscount Palmerston, was born on 20 October 1784. Surprisingly enough, he was a somewhat staid youth, good-looking but rather languid. He went to Harrow public school, then on to Edinburgh University where he studied the new subject of political economy and soaked up radical ideas. He was an 'uncommonly good' student, quiet, considerate and studious, but lacking in drive and push. Rather dull, in fact. He was fairly straitlaced at St John's College, Cambridge, too, where his social life was 'full, but by no means debauched'. He made it a rule always to be in bed by ten o'clock as he was regularly up by seven.

His father died when he was 17 and he inherited his title along with estates in Ireland. He also inherited, by arrangement, his father's old parliamentary seat at Newport in the Isle of Wight and entered the House of Commons when he was 23. Having a reasonable grasp of economics, he was offered a choice among the junior financial offices. He chose the Admiralty. It was a strictly administrative post without a seat in the Cabinet and though he became noted for his capacity for hard work he didn't trouble his head too much about politics, for the true Harry Palmerston was beginning to emerge.

Almost overnight he turned from an abstemious young prig whom girls found 'as dull as ditchwater' into something of a Regency rake. The elegantly dressed young Palmerston threw himself into social life and amorous adventures with puckish high spirits. He also became extremely feckless about paying his bills and was sued by creditors at least 20 times. He became passionately fond of clothes and assumed the air of a dandy.

When Spencer Perceval, formerly Chancellor of the Exchequer, became prime minister, to everyone's surprise he summoned 'Lord Cupid' and offered him the now vacant Chancellorship. Palmerston, who was not yet 25, hesitated. He had no great knowledge of high finance and dreaded the thought of making lengthy speeches in the House of Commons. Instead Perceval made him Secretary of War, a position he occupied for the next 20 years.

Success at the War Office, his good looks and rakish charm gained him entrée to the drawing rooms and boudoirs of fashionable England. Soon he was also the lover of three of the most famous society beauties in London.

Though mentioned frequently in society columns for his attendance at great balls, dinners and banquets, he was more at ease in the private and select atmosphere of Almack's Club in St James's. Almack's was the most snobbish and exclusive club in London, ruled by seven autocratic patronesses who had the final word as to who could or could not join. Among the seven were the Countess of Jersey, a dark-haired beauty with flawless skin and a will of iron; Madame de Lieven, wife of the Russian Ambassador, famous for her long, elegant neck and beautiful eyes, and Countess Cowper, formerly Emily Lamb, gay and vivacious sister of the great Lord Melbourne. He wooed and won them all.

Lady Jersey, proud, domineering and hated by most of the other women at Almack's, had a firm grip on Palmerston and it was thought their liaison lasted, on and off, for 25 years. Her easy-going husband, who had come into a huge fortune by marrying her, did not make a fuss about the affair. He resolutely refused to fight duels in defence of her honour. He said that if he once started he would have to fight half the male population of London.

In 1823, when he was 38, Palmerston thought it was time he married, and proposed to Georgiana Fane, Lady Jersey's younger sister, but she refused him. Lady Jersey was busy telling everybody that Palmerston was madly in love with her and for that reason would not marry her sister or anyone else. Two years later he proposed to Georgiana again at a ball at Devonshire House but she refused him again. People were convinced it was all Lady Jersey's doing and that her sister dare not say 'yes'.

When the Countess was not available Palmerston gave his attention to the fascinating wife of the Russian Ambassador. Madame de Lieven was not a conventionally beautiful woman. Some thought her nose too long and her complexion too coarse. But she had an air of mystery, was very intelligent and a skilful political intriguer. The letters between her and Palmerston indicate quite

39

clearly that they were having an affair. They waltzed together night after night at Almack's, creating shockwaves among those who still considered the dance thoroughly improper.

But it was with the third of the patronesses that Palmerston fell deeply in love. His affair with Lady Cowper was to last a lifetime, though both of them strayed into fresh pastures every now and then. She had married Lord Cowper in 1805 but they were not suited. He was a quiet, retiring man who preferred to keep himself aloof from high society. He left his wife to conduct her life as she pleased. Lady Cowper acquired the reputation of having had many lovers but her kindness and gaiety made her very popular. Palmerston sketched a cupid for her in her album and scribbled a romantic verse. His amorous activities did not end there, however. He lived with her more or less openly until their marriage in middle age and her younger children were thought to be his offspring.

As a diversion he tried his hand with Mrs Stanley, later Lady Stanley of Alderley, a beautiful woman who lived in Italy for a time and became a spirited supporter of the cause of Italian liberation. She told a friend that soon after her marriage in 1826 Palmerston had made love to her, 'in his impudent, brusque way. "Ha, ha! I see it all – beautiful woman neglected by her husband – allow me, etc.".'

Though he was widely respected for his work at the War Office, nobody liked him very much at this period of his life because of his arrogance, his high-handed manner and total lack of consideration for others. He was a firm believer in the rule of law, corporal punishment, hanging and flogging. But his great days were still to come.

Though still a Tory at heart, he crossed over to the Whigs at the invitation of Lord John Russell, who formed the last Whig government in British history. He couldn't resist an opportunity when it was handed to him on a plate. Besides, Madame de Lieven had smoothed his way by strongly commending him in the right circles. At the age of 46 he became foreign secretary. Few expected him to make a success of it, but he was dazzling.

His triumph came in 1850 with the Don Pacifico affair when he established the principle that wherever or whenever a British subject was in trouble, he had every right to expect the British government to back him to the hilt. In this case the Briton was a Gibraltar-born Jew called David Pacifico who had suffered at the hands of a Greek mob in Athens. Palmerston sent in the British navy when the Greek government refused to give Pacifico compensation and earned his reputation for gunboat diplomacy. When he defended his policy in one of the most famous speeches ever made in the House of Commons he was accorded a thunderous ovation that went on for hours.

He worked like a trojan and expected everyone else to do the same. He seldom had a midday meal but simply ate an orange to save time. His evening meal,

Lord Palmerston

Lady Cowper

however, often included seven meat courses. As foreign secretary 'Lord Cupid' still had a dashing, youthful look about him. He was trim, always fashionably dressed and sported luxurious sidewhiskers. His responsibilities gave him little time for prolonged love affairs but he fitted in casual amours whenever he could. Whenever he was late for an appointment, it was whispered that he had been making love to one of his mistresses.

Marriage to Lady Cowper did not stop his cavorting, though he was very happy with her and glad to have a domestic anchor. When her husband died she did not fling herself into Palmerston's arms immediately but kept him waiting for two years. Palmerston persisted in his proposals and her brother, the great Lord Melbourne, touched by the 'excessive niceness of his steady perseverance' advised her that, 'if you like it, to do it, not potter about it'. So in October 1839 the 55-year-old Palmerston gave up his bachelorhood and married his Emily at St George's, Hanover Square. Young Queen Victoria was said to have taken a keen interest in the wedding.

They became an immensely popular couple but notorious for unpunctuality. They never arrived on time for banquets and dinners and there was a saying in London society that the Palmerstons always missed the soup.

Palmerston himself had never cared two pins about timekeeping, leaving important visitors to kick their heels and fume at his discourtesy. Queen Victoria was almost speechless when he kept her waiting while he went for a short ride to work up an appetite for lunch. But then she hardly knew what to make of this extraordinary character. He didn't seem to care what society thought of him. She shuddered when she thought of his moral laxity, and it was only through the good offices of his brother-in-law, Lord Melbourne, that she was persuaded to overlook his scandalous attempt to seduce one of her ladies-in-waiting at Windsor Castle.

Just when Victoria thought he had mended his ways, he was reported to be in pursuit of a beautiful young Catholic widow called Mrs Laura Petre. There was some talk in Cabinet circles that he was making love to Mrs Petre instead of attending to business. But the wagging tongues were soon silenced. Mrs Petre left Palmerston to get on with his work and entered a convent where she became a prioress.

He became prime minister for the first time at the age of 70 when he had been in Parliament for 48 years and proved himself an inspired leader through the horrors of the Crimean War. Four years later he became premier for the second time. Now he was the Grand Old Man of British politics, the patriot supreme who was known affectionately to the public at large as 'Old Pam'. His figure was still trim under the buttons of his tight frock coat and he wore his hat at a jaunty angle. Apart from gout he was remarkably healthy and had an enormous appetite.

When they weren't in London the Palmerstons lived and entertained lavishly at Broadlands, later Lord Mountbatten's home, at Romsey. They were extremely informal and meals were liable to be served at any time. When cigars were lit after dinner, talk would often drift to the scandalous days of Palmerston's early love affairs and his amorous triumphs at Almack's.

But the gossipmongers still had one more delicious Palmerston tit-bit to chew over. In 1863, in his 79th year, he was cited as co-respondent in a much talked about divorce case. It appears he had been visited at his London house by a Mrs O'Kane, the wife of an Irish radical journalist. She was rather attractive, plump, with fine dark hair and beautiful eyes. According to her husband, he had sent her to see Palmerston on some political matter. Before she had been in the house five minutes Palmerston began to make love to her and, before she left, they had committed adultery. O'Kane also claimed they had met and slept together on a number of other occasions. He claimed £20,000 damages and when Palmerston hotly denied the allegations, cited him as co-respondent. Lady Palmerston laughed merrily at the whole affair and said it was just a brazen attempt to extort money. O'Kane's case finally collapsed and 'Lord Cupid' was declared to be wholly blameless. But society, intrigued nonetheless, chuckled, and continued to 'believe the worst'. Disraeli was heard to complain that the case would only make old Palmerston more popular than ever.

Dashing 'Old Pam' went out driving in his carriage one October day two years after the scandal, caught a chill, then a fever, and in spite of consuming a hearty breakfast of mutton chops washed down with port, passed on to the Upper House. Shares fell on the Stock Exchange and people began to realize that political life would be much duller without him.

Napoleon

Power meant more to him than women. That was the truth of it. But Napoleon Bonaparte had a romantic, passionate nature that could not be denied. So, in the midst of war, he could sit down and write to Josephine Beauharnais: 'Your image and the intoxicating pleasure of last night allow my senses no rest. Sweet and matchless Josephine, how strangely you work upon my heart . . . a thousand kisses, but give me none back for they set my blood on fire.'

His love for the Creole who was to become his Empress poured out in floods of romantic words, classic love letters that are still read today. But when it became necessary for him to re-marry if he was to found a dynasty, he did not hesitate to put her aside. 'Be brave,' he told the unhappy Josephine, 'you know I will always be your friend.'

Napoleon had two wives, Josephine and Marie Louise, and at least twelve mistresses. On the whole his attitude to women was tender and uncomplicated. He moved from mistress to mistress, always under the impression that he was genuinely in love.

To the end of his days he remembered every detail of his youthful idyll with Caroline Colombier at a cherry-gathering expedition in Valence in 1786. He was a young officer cadet then, barely 16, newly arrived from Corsica. She was sweet and fresh and lovely; he was thin, lank-haired and gauche. Years later he saw her face in a crowd, recognized her and greeted her with tears.

As Captain Bonaparte, already stirring with ambitions, he asked a Marseilles cloth merchant for the hand of his daughter, Désirée Clary. She was the pretty younger sister of his brother Joseph's wife. But the merchant Clary decided one Bonaparte in the family was enough. Napoleon's wooing had been tepid and Désirée, in love with the Corsican, never forgave him for his lack of determination. She was later to marry his most unrelenting enemy, Count Bernadotte, and become Queen of Sweden.

In the next few years his military career progressed swiftly. He was recalled from the Italian front in 1795 to become commander of the Garrison in Paris. When he crushed the Royalist insurrection in the capital and saved the Convention, he became a hero.

Among those who watched the Corsican with fascination was Joséphine Beauharnais. Her husband had been guillotined during the Terror and she and her two children, Hortense and Eugène, had not long been released from prison.

The 14-year-old boy asked to see Napoleon, told him he was the son of General Beauharnais and asked if he could please keep his father's sword. He returned home full of praise for Napoleon's kindness and gentlemanly behaviour towards him. Josephine invited him to call on her so that she might thank him.

Napoleon at once became a regular visitor to her small house in the rue Chantereine and fell madly in love. She was 32, six years older than him, handsome rather than beautiful, graceful, with a pleasant voice and regular features. Napoleon was still quite unsophisticated with regard to the opposite sex, but Josephine was worldly and had developed her sensual life to a fine art. The Vicomte de Barras, commander of the Army of the Interior, whose mistress she had been, advised Napoleon to marry her. The wedding took place on 9 March 1796 in a registrar's office. Napoleon was two hours late.

Barras handed him supreme command of the army in Italy as a wedding present. Their honeymoon lasted for one day then Napoleon set off for the south on a journey that would eventually end on the battlefield of Waterloo. The 26-year-old general was distraught at having to leave his beloved Josephine so soon. At every halt he made time to sit down and write to her what were to prove some of the most moving love letters ever composed. He begged her to come to him. 'If you hesitate you will find me ill . . . take wings . . . come . . . come.'

In the Italian campaign Napoleon showed the first signs of his genius in battle. The French went mad with relief. They had found a hero-leader at last. All he needed was her presence by his side. He wrote again and again but she delayed her departure until he could bear it no more and ordered her to come.

She had been enjoying her life in Paris and had no great desire to abandon the receptions and balls at which she had been fêted like a heroine. But once in Italy her eyes were opened. If she did not realize before that she had married a great man, she began to now. He was being treated like a king. Audiences with him were arranged in strict order of protocol, meals were taken in public and there was a constant coming and going of French generals and Italian nobles.

Josephine did not accompany him when he went back in triumph to Paris. She followed a month later. He was still deeply in love with her, so did not complain when she started to spend money on their house in the rue Chantereine. Later her attitude to money was to drive him almost mad with frustration.

In the spring of 1798 Napoleon announced that he was going to Egypt. It was to be 18 months before he saw Josephine again. His farewell was tender and loving.

The landing in Egypt was a success and he captured Cairo in July 1798. But while he was deeply involved in the east, Josephine had been amusing herself. She had always been promiscuous and now, lonely without her husband, she had apparantly taken a handsome young man called Hippolyte Charles as her lover. A letter from brother Joseph gave Napoleon the news. He said she was at that very moment under the chestnuts at Malmaison in a mansion she had acquired, equipped and redecorated at Napoleon's expense.

Napoleon took the news badly. 'The veil has been torn off once and for all,' he told Joseph with despair. His orgy of self-pity was broken by the sound of a merry laugh. Making inquiries, he discovered that it belonged to a petite, flaxen-haired soldier's wife called Margaret Pauline Foures. Her husband was a newly-commissioned officer and she had sailed from Toulon with him dressed in soldier's uniform. Despite the fact that she was newly-married, Madame Foures became Napoleon's acknowledged mistress in Egypt and wore a miniature of him on a gold chain round her neck.

His return to France was sudden and unexpected. Josephine heard the news while she was dining out, rushed home, dressed in her prettiest clothes and went to meet him. She wanted to explain her conduct before anyone else could get to him. But in her haste she missed his cavalcade and he reached home to find his mother, not Josephine, waiting. His family flocked around telling him of her infidelity and her wild extravagance. He promised to divorce her, rushed up to his room and locked the door.

When Josephine returned, too late, she fell on her knees, begging him to open the door so that she could be heard. He refused. Just as she was about to go away, the maid arrived with her children. Napoleon could not resist them. The door was suddenly flung open and all three were gathered into his arms.

Josephine was never again unfaithful though Napoleon himself had fleeting affairs with actresses, countesses and adventuresses, not from physical desire alone but to escape for a while from the pitiless pressures of statesmanship. He was embroiled in transitory love affairs during the pre-Austerlitz period, and was actually caught in his bedroom with Marguerite Georges, or Georgina, as he called the empty-headed little actress. For once it was Josephine who suffered jealousy.

That Josephine still meant a great deal to him was proved by his insistence on her rights during the weeks preceding their coronation as Emperor and Empress on 2 December 1804. But within two years Napoleon would ask for his freedom.

Napoleon Bonaparte

The Empress in distress

On his triumphal entry into Warsaw in November 1806 Napoleon was greeted by an 18-year-old Polish countess, Marie Walewska. She was waiting, with crowds of peasants, in the little town of Bronia between his headquarters at Pultusk and Warsaw. He only caught a glimpse of her but the impression of magnolia skin, flaxen hair and blue eyes stayed with him.

He recognized her instantly when she attended a grand ball soon after his arrival and learned that she was the wife of a 70-year-old Polish patriot. He asked her to dance but she declined. He went back to his room and wrote her a note. 'I saw but you. I admired but you. I desire but you. Answer at once and calm the impatient ardour of N'. She refused to answer this note or the notes following until he blackmailed her into submission by promising, 'Your country will be even dearer to me if you have compassion on my heart.'

She gave way to him in the end and she became very precious to him. When she told him she was going to have his child, he came to a decision. He must divorce Josephine, find a royal bride and produce an heir.

He was still very fond of Josephine. They had come a long way together and she had earned his admiration and respect. One night at dinner he broke the news to her. He wanted a divorce. She screamed and fainted and had to be carried bodily to her room. But when the day of her leaving came she made her exit with great dignity.

The way was now open for his marriage to the Archduchess Marie Louise of Austria. She was a fresh-faced princess of 18 who had been brought up in total ignorance of the opposite sex. It was said that even animals with sexual organs had been cut out of her books. Napoleon was so overjoyed at becoming a member of the Hapsburg family that he did not care about her dullness and ignorance. He was so impatient to see her that on the day of her arrival he rode out to meet her, stopped the carriage and escorted her home. The poverty-stricken court at Vienna had been amazed at the trousseau he sent and she was splendidly dressed to meet the French aristocracy.

Napoleon did not demand passion from her. He wanted a pleasant, gentle companion. Marie Louise came out of her shell, happier than she had ever thought she could be. Within a year she presented him with a son and heir, who was given the title King of Rome.

Within four years Napoleon knew that the dynasty he hoped to start with this son would never materialize. His enemies were gathering round, closing in on him. On 25 January 1814 he saw the Empress and his son for the last time. Shortly after, his downfall was proclaimed and he departed for Elba.

Josephine died of diphtheria on 29 May, 1814, and was buried at Reuil. On his last visit to Paris in a final desperate attempt to regain power he made a journey to Malmaison, visited the room where she had died and came out weeping. She had, after all, been the great love of his life. He went alone into exile.

Metternich

Metternich, powerful Chancellor of the Austro-Hungarian Empire, was the most amorous diplomat in Europe. The great peacemaker, instrumental in shaping the destiny of nations, made every woman he met fall in love with him.

He was handsome, elegant, had great wit and charm and was said to be a virile and experienced lover. Typical of his affairs was that with Princess Katharina Bagration, wife of a Russian general. One day she called on him at the legation in Dresden. They had never met before. He opened the door to find 'a beautiful naked angel' standing on the doorstep. She was wearing one of the diaphanous dresses fashionable in high society and standing against the sun she appeared to have nothing on. She was like an exquisite little marble statue. Metternich was so impressed he almost forgot to ask her in. When she looked up at him she saw a handsome fair-haired man wearing an open-necked silk shirt and a purple dressing gown trimmed with sable. In describing him afterwards she exclaimed, 'He was an Apollo descended upon Earth'. The attraction between them was so powerful that they made love at that first meeting.

Princess Katharina was highly intelligent and beautiful in a delicate oriental way. She had traces of Mongolian ancestry, seen in her high cheekbones and tilted almond eyes. Within a few weeks all Dresden knew of the affair. Even the return of his wife, Eleanora, did not make any difference to the intensity of Metternich's feelings.

Within three months the Princess knew she was going to have his child. He decided the wisest thing was to tell his wife immediately. Eleanora, who adored him, said the best solution was for her to accept the child and bring it up as their own. Metternich loved Katharina all his life, but that was the end of their affair.

Count Clemens Metternich of Coblenz was 16 when he went up to Strasbourg University in 1788. The city was full of French aristocrats fleeing from the rumblings of the Revolution. They set up their headquarters at the Inn of the Three Golden Crowns, trying to recreate the atmosphere of the Paris they had left behind. They dined, danced and gambled under vast crystal chandeliers, the women wore all their diamonds and the air was heavy with perfume.

Metternich was taken there one night. As he looked round the room one face stood out from all the rest. He could not take his eyes off Constance de la Force. She was the daughter of the Marquis de Saviale, Keeper of the Seals, one of the most beautiful women in France.

Metternich

Only 18, she was married to the Duc de Caumont la Force who left her alone a great deal. 'Who is that?' she asked as Metternich entered. 'C'est un enfant', younger even than you, her friends replied. But she insisted on meeting him.

After dinner that night she took him back to her house, pushed him into the depths of a chair and commanded, 'Wait for me.' When she next appeared it was in a white batiste dressing gown edged with soft Valenciennes lace, her small feet in white satin slippers. The champagne and her perfume overcame his senses.

THE WORLD'S GREATEST LOVERS

For the rest of his life Metternich said he sought the beauty and perfection of that night. He never found it again in quite the same way but he never stopped looking, even in old age. He wrote, 'I loved her with all the enthusiasm of youth and she loved me with all the simplicity of her heart.' The relationship lasted more than three years.

When Emperor Leopold II died, his son, Archduke Francis, succeeded him. This was good news for Metternich. The new Emperor was a good friend and only four years older than himself. He was created Minister Plenipotentiary at The Hague and sent on a special mission to England. When he returned he was a confident, accomplished, highly attractive young diplomat.

His mother, seeking a good match, chose the Countess Eleanora von Kaunitz. He was not enthusiastic, but they were married on 27 September 1795. They set up house in Vienna and Metternich profited from his wife's social position. She fell passionately in love with him, but as far as he was concerned it remained a marriage of convenience.

When he was 28 the Emperor offered him a choice of diplomatic posts. He asked for Dresden. It was a month before his wife joined him, and in that time he had had his encounter with Princess Katharina Bagration. Though his oriental charmer was never forgotten he was soon delighting in the charms of someone else. The Duchess of Kurland threw herself at him and he 'accepted her as a gift'. She was tall, beautiful, with golden ringlets and dark eyes. She proved a demanding mistress. He often tried to escape from her but she held him under her influence for a long time.

His arrival in Paris as Austrian Ambassador in August 1806 caused a great deal of interest. Metternich disliked Napoleon's politics but admired the man. The feeling was mutual. What Napoleon did not expect was that Metternich would have an affair with his sister. Caroline Murat, the Grand Duchess of Berg, who would one day be Queen of Naples, was just as stubborn as her brother when she knew what she wanted. And she wanted Metternich. She was tall, elegant and possessive. They were seen everywhere together. That did not stop him from carrying on a love affair with someone else. He was quite positive he had the ability to love one, two or even three women at the same time, saying that he cared for them all in a different way and for different reasons. So the 34-year-old dandy with his startling blue eyes, also courted the Duchess of Abrantès, a tiny feminine woman as lovely as a Dresden doll. Napoleon became very angry, fearing that Caroline had not shown enough discretion. But before the whole thing could be blown out of proportion, Metternich was recalled to Vienna with his family.

The Congress of Vienna which followed his return was the most brilliant gathering of its time, when for an entire year Vienna became the capital of Europe. Hundreds of beautiful women arrived with their husbands or families, each trying to outdo the other in elegance. But for Metternich there was only one. She was to be the greatest love of his life and her name was Julia Zichy. She was the daughter of Count Zichy, a minor courtier who had been given a post at the Congress. As Metternich got to know her he found a peace of mind and heart that he had not felt for years. She was almost nunlike in her gentle simplicity. When he craved for her physically she told him she would not become his mistress unless he promised he would have nothing more to do with other women.

Metternich was exhausted by the strenuous life he had lived ever since the first campaigns against Napoleon. He needed rest and intended to leave the Congress for a short while to recover. Julia took him to a hunting lodge in the heart of snow-covered mountains and there they walked and talked and he fell in love with her as he had with no other woman. The idea of strict fidelity appalled him at first, but he agreed. He planned a new sort of life in which they would be together for always. But the end came suddenly and tragically. Soon after the Congress Julia had turned deeply religious. She passed hours, even days, in contemplation and prayer. One day as he was sitting at the desk in his office, Metternich was handed a little box tied with black ribbon. Opening it he found ashes, charred fragments of his own love letters. Julia Zichy was dead. Metternich pillowed his arms on the desk and wept.

His wife Eleanora died, too. But he would twice marry again, from now onwards living for nothing but his family. Both his second and third wife were 20 years younger than himself, but his physical capacity remained and he was as mentally vigorous as ever. His second wife was Marie Antoinette von Leykham. He was blissfully happy with her for a year, then she died in childbirth. But the great lover still had one more triumphant love affair to consummate. He married Countess Melanie Zichy Farraris, a tempestuous, excitable Hungarian. She bore him five children. They were happy together for 22 years, then after a serious illness in March 1854 she died. 'Her last moments,' he wrote, 'might be compared with a light slowly going out.' His own light flickered and died five years later, when he was 86.

Chapter
Three

SCREEN AND STAGE

Valentino

He was the film world's first romantic idol. They called him 'the Great Lover' and up there on the screen he was certainly that. Women shrieked with ecstasy when he bared his chest in *The Sheik*. They fainted in the aisles. They read more into his performances than ever he intended. He was the lover of their dreams, the violent exciting lover who never pleaded for a woman's favours but took them as his right. 'Lie still,' he said to Agnes Ayres as he prepared to make love to her in *The Sheik*. 'Lie still, you little fool.' And every woman in the cinema wished she could take her place.

The cult of Valentino lasted for a whole generation. His Latin looks and smouldering eyes, enhanced by the costumes he wore and the brutal-tender manner in which he wooed his women, made his films box office winners.

Yet, in private life, Rudolph Valentino was nothing like the great lover women imagined. His first marriage ended on his wedding night when his bride locked him out of the bedroom. He was deeply in love with his second wife, Natacha Rambova, but she left him to pursue her career. When the sultry Polish star, Pola Negri, clinging to him like a limpet, decided she was going to be the next Mrs Valentino, he hardly noticed.

The truth was that Valentino was basically just a very likeable, Italian of peasant stock who by some strange chemistry became a star of magic sensuality on screen. After Nureyev, the great dancer and ballet idol of our own times had played the part of Valentino in Ken Russell's film of that name, he told an interviewer: 'I have watched Valentino's old films. In those days most film actors were very jittery. He was much slower, more sinuous in his movements. He would hold still and just turn his head or move his hands to indicate an emotion. There was a dance quality about his movement, which was completely natural . . .'

They knew nothing about all this in the village of Castellaneta, his birthplace in the south of Italy. To them he was Rodolpho Guglielmi, son of the local vet, the village nuisance as a child and a worry to his mother.

He was born on 6 May 1895. His father died when he was eleven and his mother urged him to learn a trade or even become a lay brother of the church when he left school. Rodolpho did not know what he wanted to do. He only knew he hated Castellaneta, its bare, stony fields, its crumbling poverty. As he entered his teens he spent more and more time wandering through the streets of the nearest town, Taranto. He probably went to agricultural college about this time but it left no impression. Taranto was like a glimpse of the outside world. His mother thought he should be content, but he was determined to see what lay beyond.

Many of the young men he met in the town talked of families who had started afresh in the New World. This, he decided, was what he would do. When he told his mother there were tears and recriminations and once, after he had thrown a violent temper, a beating from a male relative. Eventually she agreed to his emigration and sent him off with her prayers.

On 9 December 1913, Rodolpho Guglielmi joined the steerage passengers sailing for New York with dreams of a better life. As it was bitterly cold and he did not own an overcoat he stuffed sheets of newspaper under his shirt to keep warm. One American dollar was sewn into the lining of his jacket.

His first months in America shattered his illusions. He spent them living with Italian immigrant families, working as a messenger, dishwasher, janitor and shop assistant. He was desperately homesick. But in June 1914 he found work as a gardener on the Long Island estate of wealthy Cornelius Bliss. Here, something traumatic happened to him. For the first time in his life he came close to people who were rich. He became passionately interested in studying them, the way they walked, talked and laughed, the way the men devoted themselves to the pursuit of pleasure and beautiful women. One day, he swore, he too would be rich.

Perhaps he spent too much time dreaming. He lost his job on Long Island and had to take work as a gardener with the Manhattan parks department. But here, too, as he weeded and mowed grass, he watched the rich young men, copying their manners and the way they held themselves. In his leisure time he also discovered the cheap dance halls and cabarets where some of his countrymen congregated. He became increasingly skilful at popular ballroom dancing, his speciality being the continental tango. The tango was the rage of the day and no one could have been better equipped for it than Rodolpho with his dark, Latin good looks and natural grace. Soon his performance was so good people crowded round the floor to watch him.

Word spread about Rodolpho's tango and he was offered a job at Maxim's, one of the most luxurious cabarets in New York along with Delmonico's and the Ritz Grill. Cabarets of this class hired male tango dancers purely for the purpose of keeping their rich, bored women customers happy. Some of them were gigolos, living off their clients, but Valentino was always careful to point out in later years that he never became one. But he happily accepted the silk shirts, expensive toiletries and jewellery that his admirers lavished upon him. He changed his name to Rudolpho Valentina and claimed to have come from a noble Italian family which had fallen upon hard times. The rich American women he danced with loved his foreign accent, good manners and languid grace. He told them incredible stories about his past and they believed him. They shivered with delight as he held them close and brushed their ears with his lips.

Within months he was the most sought after dancer in Maxim's. The next step was to become an exhibition dancer and for this he demanded more and more professional and accomplished partners as his name became known. He had taken to wearing a corset to give him the lithe figure of a matador and he grew sideboards to emphasize the Latin look. But he was not satisfied.

He managed to get a part in a lightweight musical comedy playing its way across the country to San Francisco. When it reached Omaha, Nebraska, it died the death, but there was just enough money in the kitty to pay for coach tickets back to New York. Rodolpho exchanged his for a ticket to San Francisco.

Most of the show people he had met were talking about one thing – the movies. There were, they told him, marvellous opportunities if you were lucky, and it was all happening down there in California. Life was hard for him at first in San Francisco. He was friendless and unknown. But things looked up when he was asked to replace a dancer in a show called *Nobody Home* and made friends with a young showman called Bryan Foy.

When *Nobody Home* closed he moved to Los Angeles to share an apartment with Foy, excited by the fact that he was going to be right in the centre of filmmaking. Every day about teatime he sauntered into the Alexandria Hotel in Los Angeles where everybody who was anybody in the movie business gathered to talk shop and eat free hot ham sandwiches. He at last managed to get a couple of days work as an extra in a ballroom scene for five dollars a day, but the prospects seemed dismal.

His big break came one autumn afternoon in 1918 when he met Emmett Flynn, who had given him the job as an extra. He had liked the look of Rodolpho and suggested he play the part of a villainous count in *The Married Virgin*. Though he did not like the thought of being typecast as a foreign nasty, a gangster-cum-gigolo, he accepted. His first film roles were all the same.

During the next three years he did everything he could to improve his appearance and his image. Because of a slight physical defect – he was born with a partially cauliflowered left ear – he was turned down for the young romantic roles. Someone hit on the idea of using make-up to completely cover the ear and photographing him from the right instead of the left, but still the better parts evaded him. He learned to ride, fence, swim, play tennis, golf and bridge; he read books to improve his English and shortened his sideburns to look less Latin; had his eyebrows plucked and grew a pencil moustache. But for three years nothing went right for him.

Girls would hover round him all the time, but he had not yet learned how to deal with that sort of adulation. His first love affair was with a young actress at

Rudolph Valentino

THE WORLD'S GREATEST LOVERS

Metro called Jean Acker. It was she who suggested he should change his name to Rudolph Valentino as it was less exotic, easier to say.

Within a few days of knowing each other, they decided to get married. The wedding was a simple quiet affair with a supper party following the ceremony. Valentino, as he was now known, seemed very happy with his petite, dark-haired bride. They went to spend their honeymoon night at a Hollywood hotel where Valentino insisted on carrying his bride across the threshold of the bridal suite. But as he stooped to pick her up in his arms she stepped nimbly to one side, dashed into the room and slammed the door in his face. He laughed and knocked, asking to be let in. But Jean told him to go away, that the whole thing had been a terrible mistake. He thumped on the door, pleaded with her, begged to be let in. But she was adamant. Whatever her game was, he knew he would be a laughing stock if the story got out . . . Valentino, locked out of the bridal chamber on his wedding night! He ran from the hotel and was sick under a palm tree.

Miserable and bewildered as to why any woman would want to play such a trick – she never did give any believable reason – he accepted any parts that came his way, and continued life as a bachelor. But one of Metro's best writers, June Mathis, had been keeping a careful watch on his screen appearances and one day rang him to say she had just read a script which had the perfect part for him. It was called *The Four Horsemen of the Apocalypse*, a moving story of the 1914–18 war with most of its scenes laid in France. The president of Metro was not enthusiastic. He saw Valentino only as a young Italian dogged by bad luck. But he listened to June Mathis, whom he respected, and the part was given to Valentino.

As the daily 'rushes' were shown in the projection room, it became clear to everyone that in Valentino they had found a remarkable new star. The film itself was an artistic achievement that won columns of praise in the press but after its general release the film magazines concentrated on the young Italian. His performance inspired thousands to write asking for pictures of him, asking where he came from, when they would see him again.

Metro's barbers, masseurs and tailors had turned Valentino into a remark-ably handsome figure. Many actresses and wealthy women now asked him to spend an evening with them, often inviting him to stay the night. Remembering Jean Acker, the studios warned him of the dangers to young male actors. But he had grown weary of casual affairs and was ready for real love.

Nazimova, the famous Russian star, asked him to play opposite her as Armand Duval in the film version of *Camille*. As she had once cruelly snubbed him in public by referring to him as a gigolo he was not over anxious. But he agreed in the end for the part was too good to turn down. The set designer for *Camille* was a young woman called Natacha Rambova, a beauty, but an ice queen who liked to dominate everything and everyone. Friends told him she was the wrong woman for him, but Valentino did not listen. He could not stop talking about her beauty, her aristocratic bearing, her intelligence. It was obvious to everyone that he was hopelessly in love. His strange marriage to Jean Acker no longer upset him, but it was obviously going to pose a problem if he wanted to marry again.

On 17 January 1921 Jean Acker served notice of her suit against him for separate maintenance. She claimed he had deserted her, refused to live with her, never supported her. He threw such a monumental rage that work on the set had to stop.

When the *Four Horsemen* was generally released he found himself an international star. But the fuss that surrounded him then was nothing to what was to follow soon after.

Valentino had signed a five-year contract with Paramount and they were now wondering what to do with their new star. He was still an unknown quantity in many ways. Then Jesse Lasky, head of Paramount, had a brilliant idea. His company had recently bought a sensational novel by E.H.M. Hull called *The Sheik*. It was sensational because it had been written by a very proper English lady and told a torrid love story which included the rape of an English aristocrat by a passionate Arabian. It was rubbish, but it was a bestseller. Valentino, it was decided, should be cast as Sheik Ahmed Ben Hassan. He was thrilled. Natacha said the novel was pure trash and it would ruin his career. In fact it made him one of the screen's immortals, the forerunner of all the great screen lovers.

Valentino was a sensation. Women were advised by the film's publicity men, 'Shriek, for the Sheik will seek you too!' They gasped with shock or fainted in their seats as he swooped on Agnes Ayres, eyes burning with the flame of passion. Police had to trace hundreds of runaway girls who left home to find their own Arabian princes; women neglected their homes to see the picture again and again. Valentino himself was bemused by the intensity of this reaction. After *The Sheik* he starred in *Blood and Sand*, his lithe figure encased in the skintight costume of the matador, and once again there was a tidal wave of hysteria.

Offscreen Valentino's romance with Natacha was blooming. By May 1922 it was obvious to everyone that they would marry. Her real name, it emerged, was Winifred Hudnut and she was the stepdaughter of Richard Hudnut, the millionaire cosmetics manufacturer. On 12 May, accompanied by two close friends, the couple headed south for Mexicali, just across the border in Mexico, and were married by the local mayor. But even before they could return home there were rumours that their marriage was not valid. Valentino, who had an 'interlocutory decree of divorce' from Jean Acker, should have waited twelve months before marrying again. The seriousness of the situation was explained to

Valentino, his wife and their friend Nita Nald arriving in New York

the Valentinos by Jesse Lasky himself. Rudolph returned to Los Angeles to face the music, sending Natacha to New York to wait out the storm. Irving Shulman describes what happened next in his biography of Valentino: 'On Sunday morning, May 21 1922, Valentino, accompanied by his attorney, W.I. Gilbert, went to the district attorney's office, where he surrendered himself and pleaded guilty to a charge of bigamy before a justice of the peace. Bail was set at 10,000 dollars. Only half-following the proceedings, Valentino prepared to leave – and was stopped. His bail was 10,000 dollars. But it was Sunday, the banks were closed, and he did not carry such sums on his person. Nor did Mr Gilbert have the money at hand. Paramount officials could not or would not provide the bail in cash – as was required. Valentino was clapped into a cell.'

He beat against the bars, shouting in Italian and English, but to no avail. He never forgave Paramount this indignity. Next morning he was hurried from jail past an army of reporters. His ordeal and the subsequent decision that he should be freed of the bigamy charge brought him terrific publicity but he felt he had been humiliated and he was angry.

Natacha and Valentino were remarried in a quiet, private ceremony in Indiana on 14 March 1923, then set out on a European tour that was a honeymoon. For Valentino the voyage was a personal triumph. Ten years before he had travelled steerage as an immigrant. Now he strolled about the first-class deck looking the epitome of elegance and wealth in a magnificent overcoat with fur collar and cuffs. He was proud of Natacha whose classic, cool beauty made every head turn. Their stay in Europe was full of excitement and he indulged his greatest weakness – shopping. He purchased, among other things, a Voisin racing tourer with vermilion morocco lining; three dozen silk shirts, several dozen pairs of silk pyjamas, twelve lounging robes and twelve quilted smoking jackets. He also found time to be measured for several dozen sets of fine silk underwear.

When he returned to America it was announced that he would star in *Monsieur Beaucaire*, a costume drama that would put him into knee breeches and powdered wigs and show off his looks dramatically. As soon as it was announced thousands of women besieged the studios asking for jobs as extras. Even wealthy women offered to work as canteen waitresses just to get a glimpse of him on the set. Some offered to work without pay, others offered themselves, sending their photographs taken stark naked. There were letters pleading for just one item of his underwear, as long as he had worn it; letters beseeching him for one hour of love. Paramount publicity did its best to add to these raging fires of passion. They told lovelorn fans that Valentino had become the world's most erotic male because he spent his leisure poring over ancient books of love and from these volumes he had discovered 'the ten ways to infinite delight, indefinitely prolonged till eternity'! Valentino laughed at his publicity. Natacha did not.

THE WORLD'S GREATEST LOVERS

He had started throwing money about like a madman, buying everything and anything that took his fancy: books, illuminated manuscripts, large dogs, Persian rugs, old chests, Turkish and Arabic furniture, portraits, dinner services and antique suits of armour. Perhaps it was to take his mind off the fact that his wife was becoming a problem. Natacha fought him constantly, and evenings at home in their sumptuous hilltop mansion, Falcon Lair, became increasingly tense.

She detested his image as the great lover and always thought he should be doing something to increase his stature as an actor. She hated the crowds that pushed around him, though perhaps her aversion was understandable. One night Valentino took a girl who worked in the publicity department of United Artists to the cinema. There was pandemonium. People stood on their seats to get a better look at him. As he left the cinema his police escort was swept away by fans demanding his autograph. He was left struggling, trying to get into his limousine. One woman with a pair of scissors cut the buttons off his coat, others were tearing at his clothes, trying to stroke his hair. His bowtie was snatched off; he lost his handkerchief and scarf along with several gold studs and a glove. Both seams of his coat were torn under the arms where women had pulled at him.

When he went to Europe the scenes were repeated. At the London première of *The Eagle* at the Marble Arch Pavilion, thousands of screaming women were waiting for him and tried to tear the doors off his car. In France they ran amok as he descended from his train on a bitter December day, tearing his clothes and scratching his face.

He looked into the middle distance nowadays when reporters questioned him about his marriage. Natacha, on the other hand, was blurting out to everyone: 'Homes and babies are all very nice, but you can't have them and a career as well – if Valentino wants a housewife, he'll have to look again.' What Valentino really wanted was a home.

Reporters tried hard to find some story of passion that would go with his screen image. But though he escorted many beautiful women there was never any scandal to uncover. He learned when asked questions about his sexual prowess to smile enigmatically and say nothing. When there was an attempt to prove he was effeminate, he answered the slur by taking on his accuser in the boxing ring.

On 18 January 1926, divorce from the one woman he had truly loved was announced. Reporters who pounded him with questions were impressed by his dignity and self-control. But Valentino without a lover was unthinkable. People felt sure there must be some other woman in his life. Romantic rumours linked his name with Mae Murray after he had been seen kissing her hand in a lingering fashion, and Pola Negri, the sultry Polish star, was also placed on the short list, though Valentino said he hardly knew her.

Without Natacha, he began to spend even more wildly and sank further and further into debt. He refused to look at bills, brushing them aside impatiently, and suddenly deciding to replace everything in the house that reminded him of her. He made *The Son of the Sheik* mainly for money. Pola Negri seemed to be always hovering around him, yet it was clear the only woman he really cared for was still Natacha. He sank into deeper and deeper depressions, drove recklessly and seemed almost to be courting a quick and dramatic end. His friends, who were genuinely fond of him, pleaded with him to stop brooding and enjoy life. Pola Negri still clung to him like a limpet and talked about their undying love. But as far as Valentino was concerned, it was a one-sided affair.

There was an interval of several months before he was due to make his next film and United Artists urged him to spend the summer of 1926 in Europe where he could rest. He ordered a complete new set of luggage and a dozen new suits, then suddenly made an appointment to see Adolph Zukor to patch up his past quarrels with Paramount. Later, friends wondered if he had a feeling something was going to happen.

On Monday, 16 August, every major daily paper in America carried the news that Valentino was desperately ill. He was in hospital in New York suffering from an acute gastric ulcer and a ruptured appendix. Peritonitis had set in. Thousands of telegrams were sent to the private ward where he had been taken after collapsing in his suite at the Ambassador Hotel. Lorryloads of flowers were delivered, women wept and prayed on the hospital steps and Pola Negri retired to bed, overcome with grief. The film colony in Los Angeles was deeply shocked when it heard Valentino had had two operations and was fighting for his life. For a time he was conscious and even started to talk about making a film with Gloria Swanson.

But by the morning of 23 August 1926 all hope for him was abandoned as his condition deteriorated and he began to babble deliriously in Italian. Someone found a priest who came originally from Castellaneta and he stood at the bedside holding a crucifix to his lips. At ten minutes past noon, Valentino died. He was 31.

Scenes unprecedented in living memory took place as Valentino's body lay 'in state' at a city funeral parlour. In the end his coffin was closed and hidden. There were fears that it might be stolen.

Maurice Chevalier

Women from every walk of life adored him. 'Bonjour, Maurice!' they would shout when they saw him in the street. He was the essence of Gallic charm with his rakishly tilted straw boater, his throaty accent, his disarming smile and twinkling eye. In fact, Maurice Chevalier, probably the greatest popular entertainer France has ever produced, had the same hold over the fair sex that he had over audiences from the time when he sang in the backstreet cafés of Paris, to the Hollywood years when he was in his seventies.

The women with whom his name was associated included some of the most glamorous and famous in the world, including the legendary French cabaret star Mistinguett, Marlene Dietrich, Kay Francis and Garbo. But they all had to compete with the greatest love of his life – his mother, whom he fondly called La Louque and whom he always thought of as a saint.

His worship of La Louque was understandable when one considers his background. He was born in a Paris slum on the right bank of the Seine on the day the Eiffel Tower was lit up for the first time – 12 September 1888. His mother, a small, quiet, gentle woman, Belgian by birth, had nine children, but only Maurice, his brother Paul and another brother survived. Their father, a wine-swilling house painter, had left them to scrape an existence as best they could. They lived in a verminous, two-roomed flat, eating day-old bread because it was cheaper, and boiling bones for soup. But in her spare time La Louque earned extra money by making lace, a skill she had learned from her Flemish family. By working well into the night until her eyes were too sore to go on she was able to put away a few francs for emergencies. The strain nearly killed her. Maurice never forgot her fortitude and courage.

When Maurice's brother Paul found a job, life began to improve. La Louque even saved enough francs to take them occasionally to one or other of the café concerts in the rundown district where they lived. To Maurice, these shoddy, fifth-rate music halls were places of excitement and escape. He could think of nothing better than to be a part of them.

Somehow, at the tender age of 12, he persuaded a manager to give him a job. Billed as 'Le Petit Chevalier', he sang dubious songs full of the most appalling double entendres to audiences largely consisting of pimps and prostitutes. Made up as an urchin with false red nose and baggy trousers, he was far too innocent to understand the words. He also had to contend with heckling and shouting from drunken customers he could hardly see through a haze of cigar and tobacco smoke. But at twelve francs a week it was worth it. What he hated was having to swallow his pride and sing for three francs at the dreary little beer gardens on the outer boulevards.

By the time he was fourteen, Maurice was his mother's sole support, his two brothers having married. She meant everything to him and he would tell her all his hopes and fears. He did not, however, tell her of his lost innocence and his precocious experiences with women.

Life began to improve still more when he was signed on at the 'Petit Casino' on the boulevard Mountmarre and they were able to move to a better apartment in the place de la République. From there he got a small part in *Le Tirebouchon* (The Corkscrew) at La Parisiana, the most fashionable of the boulevard music halls. Step by step he was moving into a different world. Though his act was still based on low comedy, he knew, and everyone else knew by now, that he had just that touch of magic necessary to make him a star. He came on stage in a blue sailor's jersey, a bowler hat and baggy trousers, and when he pouted his lower lip at the girls he made them swoon in the aisles.

One night there was a sudden silence as a dazzling woman, drenched in furs, made her way to a seat close to the stage. It was Mistinguett, queen of the sophisticated revues in Paris. Maurice in turn went to see her perform. Her personality filled the theatre. She made her entrance at the top of a flight of stairs wearing sparkling shoes with incredibly high heels to show off her fabulous legs, her body sheathed in silver lamé, a towering crown of white ostrich feathers swaying on her head. Timidly, he went backstage to see her afterwards. 'How old are you, little Chevalier?' she asked in a low, throaty voice. 'I'm fifteen, Madame Mistinguett,' he replied. 'Well, listen to me,' she said. 'You've got a pretty face. You'll get to the top,' and she swept out on the arm of her current lover, little dreaming that the pretty boy would grow up to be the most important man in her life.

As for Chevalier, he lived in a trance for months afterwards. He could see quite clearly now that the coarse material he had been using was not good enough. He watched and learned from English and American entertainers, making his act more polished, funnier and more attractive to watch. Girls waited for him wherever he went and those on the bill with him either wanted to mother him or teach him the facts of life.

Mistinguett saw him at work again. She wrote in her autobiography, 'He put a song over as if he were humming to himself for his own pleasure with a rhythm and sureness of touch that took my breath away.' They met again when he visited the theatre where she was playing. 'We passed each other on the stairs,' she wrote. 'He smiled and I smiled back. He called me plain Mistinguett and I called him Chevalier . . .'

The great step forward came when he was asked to join the Folies Bergère, famous for its spectacular, daring shows and magnificent showgirls. The Folies was in a totally different class to anything he had known before. There was a constant fusillade of popping champagne corks; diamonds glittered on fashionable bosoms and the expensive smell of Havana cigars drifted on the air. He realized he had to learn polish and subtlety to conquer this world.

For a time he was madly in love with the beautiful French cabaret star Frehel. At first she mesmerized him with her perfumed sophistication, but when he realized she was leading him into the perilous waters of alcohol and drugs his native sense of caution won the day. He decided she was too dangerous and they parted company. 'My heart was bleeding,' he wrote in his memoirs, but he knew he had made the right decision.

Frehel never forgave Chevalier for leaving her. Within two years she was on the decline. Maurice had learned a great deal about women from her. He began to seek girls from a more exclusive social background and took them to nightclubs and expensive restaurants. He booked a private dining room at Maxim's, delighted that everyone turned to watch him come and go with an expensively dressed girl on his arm.

His heart lurched with excitement when he heard that Mistinguett had been booked for the 1910–11 season at the Folies Bergère. Since their meeting several years before he had never managed entirely to get her out of his mind. She was now 40 years old, 19 years older than himself, but still considered by many to be the most ravishing woman in Paris with her sleek, dark hair, enormous dark eyes and long, silky legs insured for a million francs.

Chevalier and Mistinguett were to perform an amusing sketch called 'La Valse Renversante'. In it, they played the part of lovers who quarrel, then make up, falling into each other's arms and whirling round the stage in a frenzied waltz. Their dance ended when they tumbled over a sofa and on to a rug in which they rolled themselves up. He lived for that moment when they held each other close inside the rug. One night he kissed her as they lay concealed on the stage in front of a huge audience. To his joy she responded passionately. After the show they went back to her apartment and before dawn were lovers.

Now she was 'Mist' to him and he was 'Maurice' to her. But he found, to his chagrin, that he could only meet her at lunchtimes, never at night, because she already had a man. He had to fight his rival in the street before the way was clear and he could visit her at any time in her amazing rooms high above the boulevard des Capucines.

Mistinguett, who oozed sexuality both on stage and in private, received callers reposing on a pantherskin rug beneath a flowering tree. Around the walls of her reception room were cages of singing birds. There was a huge violet sofa, a red and gold model of an eastern temple, dolls, beautiful satin cushions, photographs scattered everywhere. Her pets included a marmoset, a chattering

Mistinguett

monkey and a pair of frisky lapdogs. Through an open door could be glimpsed a vast bed with satin sheets. Beside it bottles of Mumm champagne, which she drank like water, waiting on ice.

In this exotic shrine Mistinguett taught Chevalier how to be a supreme lover, how to dress, how to behave in society. He felt ill at ease at first. His early poverty had not prepared him for this. Sometimes he resented the amount of money he had to spend. But as season followed season, they became the toast of Paris. Several times he asked her to marry him but there was a feeling in show business at that time that a star must be single to preserve his or her mystique. 'Why spoil the lovely thing we have together?' she shrugged.

Something Chevalier had not bargained for began to affect his love affair with 'Mist' – professional jealousy. Mistinguett had always chosen talented, attractive men to partner her on stage. But there was one golden rule. There must be no suggestion that they might eclipse her. Maurice, fast developing into a sophisticated performer of the first magnitude, was coming dangerously near the borderline. 'I am making you a star,' she reminded him one night. He did not like it. Perhaps it was time for him to move on professionally. Fortunately there was a brilliant new revue at the Théâtre de Cigale and a place for him to shine as a solo performer. Gone for ever were the days of red nose and baggy trousers. He performed one number in white topper and tails and had the audience on its feet. The reviews were triumphant.

War changed everything. He received his calling up papers in 1914 and was drafted into the 31st Infantry Regiment. At 26 he felt that everything was over; that he would never see the footlights again. In action he was injured by a piece of shrapnel that hit him in the chest, and was taken prisoner by the Germans. Later he was to be given the Croix de Guerre for his bravery under fire.

No news of him got through to France and rumours were rife. Some said he had been tortured or mutilated, others that he had been killed. When the censors eventually allowed him to send a brief note to his mother, it was read out to a cheering audience at the Folies Bergère. Only one good thing happened to him in the German POW camp at Alten Grabow. He persuaded a British soldier to teach him English. When a sheet of music was found he sang in English for the first time to a crowd of delighted prisoners of war. They loved his accent.

Chevalier was released early in 1916 and by 1917 was being billed at the Casino de Montparnasse, scene of some of his former triumphs. There was a moving welcome home for him but somehow he had lost his old zest. When he told Mistinguett he was troubled she shrugged her shoulders and told him he was behaving like a child. His comeback was slow and painful but he soon had people on their feet again both at the Folies Bergère and at La Cigale. The only problem was the widening gap between the lovers. The youth who had once accepted Mistinguett's imperious ways and demanding temperament had grown up during the war. He knew he deserved equal billing with her and said so. She refused to listen. 'She just thought of me as a foil, never as an equal,' he wrote later. 'I loved Mist but I adored my profession and my independence.'

They had taken a small flat in the centre of Paris, a love nest for the two of them. One day while Maurice was away Mistinguett decided to redecorate it as a surprise for him. She took an afternoon off to study colour schemes but walked in to find a pink chemise, a pair of lace trimmed knickers and a pair of silk stockings strewn carelessly on the floor. It was the beginning of the end. Chevalier always claimed that a lot of the girls he found hard to resist forced themselves on him, totally against his will. Whatever the truth, Mist's jealousy was at boiling point.

To get away from an atmosphere that was becoming more and more trying Chevalier accepted an offer to appear opposite Elsie Janis in London, taking over from Owen Nares in a show called *Hello America*. When the show finished he returned to France with a few affected English mannerisms and two trunks full of Savile Row suits. Mistinguett suspected him of having an affair with Elsie Janis and spat out 'She is a tall, chilly looking blonde. He must have had a sort of refrigerated passion for her.' After that they quarrelled incessantly. This time when Chevalier demanded equal billing the management agreed. Mistinguett walked out.

His stage appearance was now polished to perfection and thousands of women sighed over photographs of him in white tie and tails. Yet he still felt uncomfortable, as though he had not found himself. In his biography of Chevalier, Michael Freedland describes what happened next: 'One night, eyeing himself in a mirror before going to an after theatre party he thought, 'Why not a dinner jacket?' He had never seen anyone appear on stage in a dinner jacket before but, by now, he was confident. Then, one day he saw some young blades in the street, one of them leaning against a wall with a straw boater, red ribboned, jauntily tilted over one eye. That was it! He added the boater to the dinner jacket and the image of Chevalier was born.'

Now it was all over with Mistinguett, he amused himself with the pretty showgirls who crowded round him all the time. Typical of his affairs was that with a dark-haired, vivacious dancer called Simone. She crept up to him in the wings as he left the stage one night and told him sincerely, 'You were wonderful'. He suggested supper after the theatre and for a time they were seen everywhere together. She was very young, very high spirited, very fond of nightlife and champagne. Most evenings after a performance they would go out to dance till dawn.

At this time, Chevalier was filming, appearing on stage every night and at matinées and drinking too much in an attempt to keep going. Only a handful of people knew that he was on the verge of a nervous breakdown. The parting with

Maurice Chevalier and his wife arriving at Victoria Station

Mistinguett had much to do with it, but fortunately, as the frivolous Simone scampered away, the sort of woman he most needed was waiting.

Yvonne Vallée had been his leading lady for some time and, though he had never noticed it, she was deeply in love with him. Now, off stage, he began to appreciate the charm of her smile, the warmth in her deep brown eyes and a certain serenity that soothed him like a balm. Yvonne helped him through a breakdown that could have cost him his career and gave him a feeling he had never experienced before – contentment.

They set up house together at Vaucresson, a pleasant, wooded neighbourhood outside Paris. Chevalier was over his crisis and back on top form. It was now he found a risqué little song that would be associated him for the rest of his life – 'Valentine' – or 'Val-on-teen-ah' as he sang it in a sexy sort of growl. Everybody wanted to hear it.

On 10 October 1927, Maurice and Yvonne were married in the little church at Vaucresson and moved into a villa at St Cloud which they called 'Quand on est Deux' (When One is Two) after their most famous duet. They were a handsome couple, always dashing off from Paris to the Côte d'Azur. On one trip Maurice found a little place called Bocca in the hills above Cannes. He fell in love with it and bought a farmhouse and some land there, calling his new property La Louque after his mother.

They had moments of great happiness together, sitting under the bougainvillea and watching the sun go down over the sea. But Yvonne soon began to realize that marriage would never make any difference to Chevalier and he could never put aside his role as a great lover. Once they had got over the shock of his wedding, the girls were back like bees round a honeypot and his ego was ready for their adulation.

The sad truth was that Yvonne had already played her part in his life. When he thought they were going to have a child she meant everything to him. But the child was lost. Her role as healer and comforter was over, and the marriage became empty.

No one would have guessed that anything was amiss as they embarked together on the maiden voyage of the French liner *Ile de France* bound for America on 28 June 1928. Chevalier was off to Hollywood, having signed a contract with Paramount, and hundreds of women fans packed the quayside to wish him luck. He posed for pictures wearing fashionable plus fours, his arm around Yvonne, who smiled brightly under her Chanel hat.

Chevalier loved America once he got over his initial screen fright. He was an enormous success, especially after being presented with a song called 'Louise' which suited him to perfection. As he crooned 'Every leetle breeze seems to wheesper Louise' every woman within hearing curled up her toes.

His French boater, his pouting lower lip, his accent were copied everywhere.

THE WORLD'S GREATEST LOVERS

He made films with stars like Jeannette MacDonald and Claudette Colbert and surrounded himself with all the trappings of stardom. Yvonne lived in luxury and watched helplessly.

While he was shooting *Playboy in Paris*, the sensational Marlene Dietrich was making *Morocco* with Gary Cooper on a nearby set. Their dressing rooms were next door to each other. Chevalier was fascinated by her allure, her elegance and professional skill, and delighted when her cool 'Hello M. Chevalier' turned into 'Bonjour Maurice'. They visited each other in their dressing rooms after the day's shooting and laughed loud and long at each other's jokes. Hollywood buzzed with rumours about them especially when, as a prank, they appeared together in public wearing identical black suits and white scarves. He called her affectionately 'Marlinou' and bought her an emerald.

During filming one day the event he had long dreaded actually happened. La Louque died while he was far away from her. His brother Paul's telegram was delayed and he could not even reach France in time for her funeral. He locked himself into his suite at the Astoria in New York and lost himself in grief. 'Everything I did was for her,' he told friends.

After a trip back to Paris he returned to America without Yvonne, but when she heard he was being consoled by Marlene Dietrich she took the first available ship and followed him. Though Yvonne found it hard to believe, Maurice and Marlene had turned into just good friends. She amused him with her wit and touched him with unexpected acts of kindness, but that was all. The friendship lasted and in 1945 was to bring from her a moving gesture of loyalty for which Chevalier was for ever grateful.

Even the divine Garbo was not immune to his charm but their encounter was quite comic. Dancing together one night at a party, she asked him suddenly 'Do you know how to swim?' 'Mais oui,' he replied, somewhat baffled by the turn of conversation. 'Then let's take a dip in the ocean right now,' she suggested. 'But it's midnight,' protested Chevalier. 'Le Pacifique est glacial!' Garbo gave a snort of derision and stalked off the floor. So much for romantic Frenchmen.

He returned to Europe, billed as the highest paid entertainer in the world, to appear at the Dominion Theatre in London. When he arrived at Victoria Station his car was besieged by frantic women. Reporters wanted to know his secret as a great lover, 'I do not look upon myself as a great lover,' he told them. 'I just want to make people happy. Mind you, the fellow who can make a pretty girl laugh . . .'

From now on he divided himself between France and America. Paris he always thought of as home but he loved New York and Hollywood because they stimulated his talent. Yvonne, however, could no longer stand the attention paid to him by all the beautiful women in the film industry. She announced she would sue for a divorce. Sadly, towards the end of their marriage they had nothing to say to each other.

Kay Francis, the dark seductive actress who often played opposite William Powell, was the next woman in his life. For a time his affair with her was a spirited one but she was moody and friends could tell the state of their relationship by the happiness or despair on his face. She remained something of an enigma. Another affair going on that would have caused a scandal if it had been made public at that time was with Josephine Baker, the beautiful coloured dancer.

Then, quite suddenly, at the age of 46 Chevalier fell genuinely in love with a 19-year-old Jewish girl. He first saw her in a Paris edition of the New York hit *Broadway*, asked for an introduction and was taken backstage to meet her. Pretty, dark-haired, with curls close to her head and teasing dark eyes, she was the type he found hard to resist. Her name was Nita Raya and she was of Rumanian stock. He was fascinated and saw her day after day. He found she aroused in him a passion he had thought was on the wane.

But was he doing wrong? He was very worried about the difference in their ages and even took the unusual step, for him, of going to church to confess and seek guidance. Still unconvinced he decided that he could permit himself this love if he made one big sacrifice. He stopped smoking. He followed that by denying himself alcohol and rich food. Though his physical health improved enormously, his conscience remained uneasy. Finally he decided to tell Nita that the affair must come to an end. She wept so bitterly that he relented and promised to set up house with her.

When war broke out in 1939 he went to ground for a while at La Bocca, taking with him Nita and her elderly parents. He then made what most of his friends considered the worst mistake of his life. He decided to return to Paris after the Germans had taken over. Many people, including his great friend Charles Boyer, urged him to flee and join the Free French in England. But Maurice was a totally unpolitical animal, almost naïve in these respects. He could only think that he ought to stay with his countrymen, stay with the Paris theatre. After all, would the French have him back if he deserted now? Many of his actions were to be misinterpreted. Members of the resistance were filled with anger when they saw the greatest entertainer in France performing for Nazi officers. Later, he was to remind people that the woman he loved was a Jew. If he showed any sign of hesitation when he was asked to perform by the Nazis they would remind him that his mistress and her parents were very vulnerable.

The word 'collaborator' was thrown at him as the war ended and he had to appear before a 'purification committee' before being declared innocent. He felt he could never sing again and lapsed into a period of depression. When he felt at his lowest, one of the beautiful women from his past appeared like a saving angel. It was Marlene Dietrich, looking incredibly chic in military uniform. 'Noel

THE WORLD'S GREATEST LOVERS

Coward and myself are singing at the Stage Door Canteen,' she told him. It's time you got back to work, too. Come and join us.' Some of the French performers on the bill protested. They said they would not work with a collaborator. Dietrich said they would not appear unless Chevalier was with them. The act of loyalty hauled him out of his post-war trauma.

His hair was streaked with grey now, but it merely enhanced his mature good looks. On stage his old magic began to work again and he announced he was at last going to marry Nita. Congratulations poured in, but the engagement was suddenly called off. Perhaps his proposal had been left too late. Nita had been with Maurice for 12 years and on the brink of making things legal between them she had the urge to take up her career again, to feel independent. He let her go with good grace, even found her a flat in Paris and helped her professionally.

A girl called Françoise consoled him. Women still enjoyed being swept off their feet by the great Chevalier and, as he said with a shrug: 'You've got to be so cold not to get a shock when you see a really attractive woman.' As he grew older he did not, he said, allow himself the luxury of passion. 'If I do, it will not be good. Or it will be worse – sad.' It was agreeable, he said, just to look at youth and bask in its admiration. Long experience had taught him how to conduct a relationship with great subtlety and how to end an affair so that his partner would remember him with affection.

But after 55 years in show business and almost as many as a great lover, was it not time to bring down the curtain and sink into gentle retirement? In Paris people were certainly beginning to take him for granted and there were often empty seats at his shows. But he was still full of vitality and eager for new offers. He decided to take a trip to America, the country that had always given him big chances.

Booked for a season at Ciro's nightclub, his twice nightly performances were a huge success. One night Vincente Minnelli, the Hollywood director, was in the audience. After the show he went backstage to see Chevalier. He asked if he would be interested in taking a starring role in a film he was going to make. It was based on a story by Colette, a story called 'Gigi'.

Afterwards Chevalier said some of the happiest moments of his life were spent making that film. The part was made for him. The songs written for him by Alan J. Lerner were some of the most enchanting he had ever performed. He stole the show with 'I'm glad I'm not young any more' which Lerner wrote after Chevalier had talked to him about life and getting older.

Now in his seventies, he fell in love for the last time. Janie Michel was a brilliant young red-haired artist who had been a pupil of Matisse and was already married to the Comte de la Chapelle. She found herself drawn to Chevalier and he found he could talk to her as he had to no one else, telling her how close he had come once to taking his own life and how bitterly the word 'collaborator' had weighed on his heart. Their relationship was discreet and Janie had a wonderful effect on him.

Films like *Gigi* and *Love in the Afternoon* had introduced him to a whole new generation. He was delighted with his impact and the knowledge that with his white hair, tanned complexion and trim, upright figure he could still break a few hearts. On his 72nd birthday in 1960 he was asked what he felt about the advancing years. 'Considering the alternative,' he said, with his wicked, Gallic chuckle, 'Not too bad, not too bad at all.' He still had several pictures to make, including *Fanny* with his old friend Charles Boyer. Janie often went on location with him.

Chevalier, the music-hall favourite

He had made over his property at La Bocca to the French performing rights society as a home for elderly performers and had bought himself a huge, rambling house in the little village of Marnes la Coquette, near Paris. It was to this house he retreated when, on 20 October 1968, he left the stage for the last time after 68 years of show business. Janie saw a change come over him. He could not live without the footlights, without applause. Gentle melancholy descended on him. He dined often with the Duke and Duchess of Windsor and took elegant women like Suzy Volterra to the races. But he was homesick for the stage. Gradually he retreated more and more into his own home and there were signs that his general factotum, Felix Paquet, was trying to dominate him, keep him from his friends and even from Janie.

A few years earlier he had heard that Mistinguett had died lying on a satin bed surrounded by violets and azaleas and he wrote: 'In the final reckoning no one else has ever been what she was to me or done for me what she did. More than any other woman she was what I mean by love.'

Now, after a short, sad period in which his health failed and he seemed to feel that life was not worth living any more, he died from a heart attack on New Year's Day, 1972. He was 83. They laid him to rest beside the woman who had really meant more to him than all the rest, more even than Mistinguett – La Louque.

Mae West

That high priestess of hussies, Mae West, once said that getting down to your last man was as bad as getting down to your last dollar. As the opulent forerunner of Hollywood's golden goddesses, Miss West, as she insisted on being called, also claimed she knew more about the opposite sex than would fit into an encyclopaedia. She proved it by issuing salty aphorisms about men nearly every time she opened her mouth.

She owned up to many lovers, the odd duke and a few oil tycoons among them, but when asked how many retorted, 'The score never interested me, only the game.' She avoided any scandal in her private life, which was conducted with surprising restraint. She neither smoked nor drank, refused to name her 'gentlemen friends' and seldom appeared in public with more than one at a time.

Her most famous line, 'Come up and see me some time', delivered with a lascivious wink and the lift of a white shoulder, did not have to be taken too literally. Mae West did not insist on being called Miss West for nothing. Her famous image – blonde curls, a voluptuous figure squeezed into a tube of sequins, lilting nasal voice and the arch smile of a temptress – had been carefully and cleverly built up over the years.

Mae West was born in Brooklyn in 1892. She got her blonde looks from her mother who was of Franco–German stock. Her father was a prize fighter. She must have been precocious, for her parents put her into stock drama at the Gotham Theatre, Brooklyn, when she was only five years old. Too young to read theatre scripts, she had them read over to her and learned them by ear, a habit she kept all her professional life. At 14, with a fast ripening figure and a twinkle in her eye, she suddenly emerged as a juvenile vamp in skintight black velvet and paste diamonds. About this time, too, she discovered that girls were a waste of time and boys much more interesting.

She married Vaudeville actor Frank Wallace in 1911 when she was 18 years old but domesticity and children did not fit in with the personality she was developing for herself. Their relationship did not last. Much later in life she said, 'I was sorry about Frank, but I was not in love with him. It was just one of those things. I should never have married him. But having made one mistake in marriage, I vowed I would never make another.' Instead she found safety in numbers. 'The recurring pattern of multiple men in my life was already showing itself. I start with one and usually five or six more put in an appearance.'

Miss West had developed her personality a little too far, according to the police. After years appearing in other people's shows she put on a play herself in 1927 at Daly's Theatre on Broadway. It was called simply *Sex*. It ran for a year before the powerful puritan element in New York managed to have Miss West hauled up on an indecency charge and jailed for ten days for 'corrupting the morals of youth' – largely because of a low life scene, realistically depicted. She felt she had suffered a grievous wrong, and said so. The trouble was she could not now speak a line without people looking for a double meaning. She delivered every word with such superb insolence that everyone felt there must be more to what she said than appeared on the surface. Defiantly, she followed *Sex* with several more risqué plays, continuing to treat life with irreverence in such masterpieces as *The Wicked Age, Pleasure Men* and *The Drag*.

She reached the pinnacle of fame in the 1930s, invading Hollywood to play screen hussies with names like Peaches O'Day and Klondyke Annie. Her dresses were skintight, designed to show off her splendid bosom, and worn with enormous hats and diamond earrings like chandeliers. She batted eyelashes a yard long as she drawled her cynical wisecracks through insolently curved scarlet lips. 'A girl has to look out for herself,' she confided to her audience. 'A full moon and a wireless set, without a man, is just so much consolation.'

Mae West

Surprisingly, many of her wisecracks were spontaneous, not studied. Asked in an interview if she had any formula for getting her man, she returned crisply, 'Girls don't like formulas.' Her most famous line, 'Come up and see me some time' occurred in a film called *She Done Him Wrong* made in 1933, but almost equally memorable was her quip, 'When I act I don't make love and when I make love I don't act' – the last word spat out like a plum stone.

Off screen and in private the hipswinging flamboyance was left behind. She looked smaller, prettier, with violet eyes, platinum blonde hair and an arched upper lip that gave her a girlish look. Her honesty made her popular among her fellow stars in Hollywood. She hated getting up early. Callers and telephone calls were barred before noon. Then she would dress herself with absolute care and put on her jewellery – a platinum and diamond bracelet with 17 gold charms, a 200-carat sapphire ring, diamond earrings that caught every light in the room. She literally dripped with diamonds, admitting that most of them had been given to her by admirers. At one time her jewels were estimated to be worth a quarter of a million pounds.

She loved the colour peach. She bought peach underwear, peach satin sheets, and decorated the dressing room and living room at her famous studio bungalow in peach and cream. Her best known luxury was a huge, swan-shaped bed, smothered in silk and lace, with overhead mirrors reflecting 19th-century opulence.

Mae West said she had never knowingly allowed a married man to make love to her. One look at a wedding ring and she cooled off. 'But sometimes,' she admitted, 'it seems to me I've known so many men, the FBI ought to come to me for fingerprints.'

Men improved when they got to 40, she said. 'At 40 a man has come of age. He has more polish, poise, charm and more money. Money buys time, place, comfort and a private corner for the two of you to be alone. A man has more character at 40, too. He has suffered longer and the more suffering, the more character.'

Miss West wrote down a lot of this philosophizing about the opposite sex in a book she called *Goodness had nothing to do with it*, in which she gave advice to women on how to succeed in her line of business. 'I never set out to make men a career,' she drawled. 'It just happened that way. I had a certain something for them and the word got around . . .'

So she became rich, successful and popular. But the puritan community in America, consisting largely of church groups and women's committees, incensed by her attitude to sex, were waiting to catch her out. Their opportunity came in 1938 when she took part in a broadcast burlesque skit called 'Adam and Eve'. She played the part of Eve and Don Ameche was Adam. In the script Adam is made to appear cool towards Eve until the serpent gives her an apple from which she makes apple sauce. This raised a storm of protest and was described by Bible students as 'obscene, indecent and scurrilous'.

'I wouldn't do anything to hurt religion. I go to church myself,' pleaded Miss West. 'I know what's vulgar and what isn't,' she exclaimed. 'I make fun of vulgarity but people insist on getting me wrong.'

The protesters complained that it was not so much what she said but the way that she said it. 'I can't help my voice,' she retorted. Everyone enjoyed the scrap, and she went on from strength to strength.

During the Second World War her name entered the language. The lifejacket worn by airmen in combat was named after her. Her great creation was the character 'Diamond Lil', which she played on Broadway, on the screen and in theatres all over the world. She wrote, produced and appeared in it and though the critics gave mixed reviews no one denied her impact as a larger than life character.

She retired from films when she was 63 to live in her palatial beachhouse overlooking the Pacific at Santa Monica. At 70 she kept pretty much to herself, scorning drink, tobacco and Hollywood. When at last she gave an interview to the *Saturday Evening Post*, after people had been trying to talk to her for years, she received the reporter in her bedroom in full regalia – a pink satin négligée, blonde wig, false eyelashes and diamonds. 'Miss West still possesses overwhelming sexual force,' wrote the reporter. 'It comes and goes like distant music heard across a fairground on a summer night – but it is still there.'

Errol Flynn

Errol Flynn was a man out of his time. He was a pirate, a buccaneer, a swashbuckling rake who, according to his own highly coloured account of himself, had tasted every vice from Macao to Marseilles. He was a lover of Olympic stature, a seducer and, when it suited his purpose, the most gloriously inventive liar. But he was always completely honest with himself.

This latter day Casanova, one of the most colourful characters ever to come out of the film industry, did everything to excess. Women loved him and men laughingly envied and liked him.

In his prime Flynn was a beautiful man with a magnificent deeply tanned physique, well-cut features and deep blue eyes full of laughter and devilment.

He was always in the middle of some fantastic tangle involving either women, drink or fighting.

He always styled himself as an Irish Tasmanian. Born in Hobart, Tasmania, in 1909, he was the son of an eminent biologist, Professor Theodore Thomson Flynn. His mother, said Errol, considered him a very nasty little boy and an even nastier big one, for at 16 he nearly killed another youngster in a fight and was expelled from school.

Work was found for him in a local office but he was sacked when he was discovered dipping into the petty cash for money to bet on horses. There were to be no more office jobs for Flynn. News of a gold strike in New Guinea fired his imagination and at 17 he set out to make his fortune.

The story of the next five years, told in his autobiography *My Wicked, Wicked Ways*, reads like an impossible film script.

First he bluffed his way into the colonial service as a sanitation inspector. Thrown out of that job after being caught in the arms of a high official's wife, he then talked his way into being made manager of a copra plantation. The money was good and soon he had enough to buy a schooner in which he ran freight and passengers along the coast. Twice he tried for a strike in the gold fields, but each time he failed. His greatest success was with the local girls who were stunned by his good looks and devil-may-care ways. But fighting was in his blood and he became known as a tough customer, especially after being hauled before a local court for the alleged murder of a native. He barely escaped prison.

As he had had no luck with the gold and was under constant surveillance after his court appearance, he decided to head back to Australia. In Sydney he took a bizarre job as a 'sniffer' in a bottle factory, sniffing bottles to make sure they were not tainted. As this did not provide him with enough money to live well, he swallowed his pride and became a gigolo. His wealthy, middle-aged mistress, he admitted, 'woke my understanding of the possible wonder and diversity of the female form'. One night he slipped away with all her jewels, leaving a note of apology. He had decided to be an actor and needed the fare for Europe.

After a journey filled with garish incidents, he eventually arrived in London. Though he had no experience he talked Northampton repertory company into giving him a chance as a juvenile and then, by sheer good fortune, landed a bit part in an English film. By now, his hair bleached by the sun, skin the colour of mahogany and his lop-sided grin showing perfect white teeth, his physical appeal was dazzling. Jack Warner, the Hollywood film maker, saw him in the bit part and realized the potential of this beautiful young man. In no time he was off to America.

In 1935, at the age of 26, he burst upon the screen in spectacular fashion as 'Captain Blood' and for the rest of his life made millions playing similar swashbuckling costume parts. There were a few exceptions, including a film about the Second World War in which he saved Burma singlehanded.

They called him 'the Baron' and he lived up to his name by building a mansion and buying a yacht. He kept both of them unusually well stocked with pretty girls. He had already been singled out, however, by a glamorous French actress called Lili Damita, a star of second rank who earned his admiration by her 'boudoir art'. One night she stood on a window sill, several floors up, and threatened to jump if Flynn would not marry her. He understood and admired that sort of bravado and laughingly agreed. They divorced six years later and she was to cost him a great deal of alimony.

Lili told the divorce court judge that Flynn paid more attention to his yacht than to her. Or could it be the crew that took up his attention? There were always plenty of willing, lissom young women ready to go sailing with him and cook delicious little suppers before they snuggled into his bunk. His taste for teenage girls got him into trouble on several occasions. His yacht *Zaca* became forbidden territory as far as the mammas of nubile 16-year-olds were concerned.

He met his second wife, Nora Eddington, in 1945. She was small, red-haired, dynamic and determined. She took a job selling cigars in a kiosk so that she could get a chance to talk to him. He was intrigued by her and they were married that year. Flynn's roistering lifestyle proved too much, however, and it didn't last.

Flynn, of course, thoroughly enjoyed flouting convention. He didn't give a damn what anyone thought of him and chose like-minded fellow actors for his companions. But there was a side of him which many did not know. He had a lively and questing mind and read deeply. His academic father, who was very close to him, saw him quite differently to most people. He saw him as an adventurer who lived the kind of life many men would give their eye teeth for and believed him to be basically kind, intelligent and brave.

He was engaged for a time to 20-year-old Rumanian Princess Irene Ghika and they planned a spring wedding in the Greek Orthodox Church, but the romance petered out. They were not meant for each other.

He would have hated life among the minor European royals. He was happier sailing round the ports of the Mediterranean, meeting up with old friends like David Niven and Peter Finch and roaring the night away drinking vodka and reminiscing. He always said that among his fondest memories were the number of times he had ducked alimony and the night he kicked Hedda Hopper, the vitriolic Hollywood columnist.

During the latter part of his life, Flynn discovered two great loves: Jamaica, and this third wife, Patrice Wymore.

His love affair with Jamaica began in 1947 when he was forced by bad weather to put into harbour there. He thought he had found paradise. For the first time he really felt that he wanted to put down roots. He bought an estate for £33,000 and for ten years his parents helped him to run it. He needed to make regular visits to America but he regarded New York as a violent place and got away from it as fast as he could. Hollywood had become 'total anathema' to him over the years but he was realistic enough to know he had to make his living there.

It was on the set, making a film called *Rocky Mountain*, that Errol Flynn met Patrice Wymore, the beautiful red-haired actress who was to be his third and last wife. He said she was the only woman he really loved. They were married in October 1950 and she had 'seven wonderful years' with him before he drifted off again.

Though she looked elegant and lady-like she had enough spirit to join with him in his hectic lifestyle. She was seldom surprised by anything he did. Once Flynn bought a new Jaguar car and was so excited he could hardly wait to show it to her. He zoomed round the corner where they lived and yelled for her to

Errol Flynn and Patrice Wymore being married in Nice

come out. 'I'll take you for a spin round the block,' he said. They got back ten days later. Instead of going round the block, he headed for Mexico. 'In each year with him I packed in more fun, more real living than some wives get in forty years,' she said without bitterness when he had gone.

By the late fifties he was drinking vodka at the rate of a bottle a day and had got himself into the news by joining Fidel Castro for five hair-raising days behind the Cuban rebel lines in the war against Batista. He was asked whether the rumours that he had given up drinking after his experience were true. 'Malicious gossip!' roared Flynn.

He was only fifty when he died in Vancouver. He had gone there to sell his yacht *Zaca* as plans were going ahead for a house in Jamaica. He had a heart attack on the morning of 15 October 1959 and died in the hotel. He was not alone. His latest girlfriend, a pretty young starlet called Beverly Aadland, was by his side. Patrice Wymore wept bitterly for him. She said there was a sadness about him as the swashbuckling started to come to an end. And a tragic realization in his eyes that he'd thrown so much away.

Beerbohm Tree

In an age which prized respectability above all things, the great actor-manager Sir Herbert Beerbohm Tree led a double life, producing a total of ten children, only three of them legitimate. 'All Herbert's affairs start with a compliment and end with a confinement,' said his long-suffering wife Maud acidly. One of the children he fathered out of wedlock was famous cinema director, Sir Carol Reed, who kept his parentage a secret till his death. Actor Oliver Reed is also a descendant.

All his life Tree found the sight of a pretty woman irresistible and confessed himself slave to his sense of beauty. He was a fascinating man, tall, red-haired with a fine head and the most extraordinary eyes, expressive and alert, changing from pale turquoise to deep blue according to his mood. He also had a memorable voice. 'It was soft, purring, slightly nasal,' said Hesketh Pearson in his memoirs. 'The eyes and the voice combined, focused on any woman he was interested in, were enough to make the poor female putty in his hands.'

Herbert Tree succeeded Henry Irving as leader of the theatre in England. But, unlike Irving, his interests were not confined to the stage. Acting was not his whole existence. He was a many-sided man who took great delight in the social round, enjoying life to the full, talking, riding, painting, listening to music and perhaps above all, lovemaking. He dominated the theatre by the force of his personality and the vivid quality of his imagination. He captured women by his gallantry, his zest for life and his flamboyance.

His background gave him a slightly exotic, foreign touch. The Beerbohm family were Germans who came to England from Lithuania. His father, Julius, arrived in London in 1830 at the age of 20, set up as a corn merchant and married an Englishwoman, Constantia Draper. Herbert was born at Pembridge Villas in Kensington on 28 January 1852. He was brought up partly in English schools, partly by German tutors in Thuringia, an experience which set him against formal education for the rest of his life.

Because he loved his father and wanted to please him, Herbert joined the family firm at the age of 17 and tried hard to become interested in the business of selling corn. He lasted for eight years before admitting that he was bored to tears. During his leisure hours he had found his true vocation. The man who was to found the Royal Academy of Dramatic Art was teaching himself the rudiments of acting on amateur stages.

Contemporary fashion in the theatre demanded that a young actor should be dark and good looking with a noble, cleancut profile. Herbert, with his pale skin, red hair and strange blue eyes, could not have been further from that image, but he was so determined to go on the stage that eventually his father was convinced of his seriousness and gave him his blessing. Julius Beerbohm, however, pointed out that the acting profession was only acceptable if his son aimed for the top of the tree. Herbert assured his father this was where he intended to be and took the name Tree to remind him of his goal for the rest of his life.

In the spring of 1878 he made his first professional appearance with a touring company at Folkestone. Love problems were already cluttering his life but he worked hard, always studying every aspect of a character before putting it on the stage. Because of his slightly exotic air he was constantly cast as foreign counts, princes and charlatans. There were occasional successes in London, but at that time no one could have forecast his brilliant future.

He had already had plenty of proof of his ability to fascinate and attract women when he met Maud Holt in 1881. She was a pretty young thing, 18 years old, slim and blonde, with a curly fringe. They were introduced at a fancy dress ball and he discovered to his surprise that she was something of a highbrow. She taught Greek, Latin and mathematics at Queens College, Harley Street, and intended to go on to Girton. Meeting Herbert changed the course of her life. Suddenly face-to-face with this intriguing man who transfixed her with his eyes and caressed her with his voice, she was lost. She took to haunting Garrick Street in the hope of bumping into him as he came out of the Garrick Club. The encounter never took place so she wrote to him to ask his opinion as to whether or not she should go on the stage. She had, she said, already played Ophelia and Beatrice in amateur productions of Shakespeare. He replied that she certainly should not go on the stage unless she felt she *must*. To emphasize the point he went to see her at her rooms in Orchard Street. They read poetry together and she sang to him. Herbert soon had enough of that and made a passionate advance. She demurred as any decent Victorian girl would, and a year after their first meeting, her strategy was rewarded. He asked her to be his wife.

Though they stayed together for the rest of their lives, the course of their love never ran smooth. For one thing Maud, beneath her exterior of sweetness and light, was a strong-willed young lady with a strong streak of puritanical disapproval and a determination to get her own way. She soon found out that Herbert Tree was not the sort of man to be managed. When she taxed him with rumours she had heard about his life before they met he ticked her off tenderly: 'I was foolish . . . perhaps weak . . . but not vicious or dishonourable . . . you must understand that when I first asked you to care for me, my past life had not been entirely unworldly.'

Their engagement was stormy. Maud could not help noticing the way in which women were attracted to Herbert. He had a way of making them feel more alive. He gave the impression that there was no time to be lost, that each day, each hour must be lived to the full. When he was away from her he wrote lyrical letters. In one he described 'the sun setting in the west, lighting up little clouds with bright gold and crimson; the ploughed fields, purple, the corn, gold, and the landscape lighted here and there with the sun's last rays; above, a glimpse of the last blue sky . . .' He asked her to come to him as soon as possible so that he could ride with his dearest into such a sunset. Maud replied that was all very well but she was not at all pleased to hear that he had been keeping undesirable company. He had received her note, he said, and was somewhat surprised at the tone his heart's darling had used . . .

So the fencing went on, but in spite of it all they were married on 16 September 1882. From the start Herbert proved himself an adoring and attentive husband, though this did not stop him from taking advantage of Maud's briefest absence to revert to his bachelor ways. Maud spent money like water but he never complained. She always looked exquisite and made their social life a huge success. They were among the most handsome couples in England.

While Maud indulged her love of luxury, Herbert went on to carve out a great career for himself, becoming an actor-manager, first at the Comedy Theatre in London, then taking over the Haymarket in the autumn of 1887. He shrewdly sensed that the theatre public was changing, that he had to cater not only for the gentry but for the new young suburbans who were increasing in number year by year. He put in electricity, cut prices, abolished many of the oldfashioned boxes and put on spectacular productions of incredible splendour and beauty.

Every time he took a step forward Maud insisted they needed a bigger and better house. They entertained in great style, dined with the aristocracy and spent weekends in opulent country houses. Maud found a mansion for them in Hampstead with three acres of garden and coaxed Herbert into buying it by describing the idyllic summers they would have pruning their roses. Herbert let Maud have her way. He had other diversions.

He visited a Miss Carew at 13 Shrewsbury Road, Bayswater, with the idea of giving her a part in one of his productions. Their conference was no doubt quite eventful for beside the entry in his diary recording their meeting was a lovingly pressed flower.

About this time, too, Herbert must have started his fruitful liaison with Beatrice May Pinney. She later changed her name to Reed by deed poll. How he came to meet her remains a mystery, but she had some quality that kept him attached to her for the rest of his life. Perhaps she gave him domestic contentment. Very little is known about the lady beyond the fact that she was born on 23 May 1871 in the seaside town of Ramsgate and that her father was a professor of music. She gave Herbert five sons, including Carol Reed, and one daughter. Four of the children were born at Daisyfield, a house once visited by Beatrix Potter, situated in a quiet, leafy part of London where Wandsworth verges on Wimbledon Common. No one was ever quite sure whether Maud knew about her or not. One thing is certain. Herbert adored all his children – the three daughters belonging to Maud and his second, secret batch.

If he had not wandered off so persistently Maud might have been able to forgive him. He had affairs, he said rather feebly, because he could not bear to hurt a woman's feelings. He seemed to be incapable of fidelity though he was always kind and generous to the women in his life.

What held Herbert and Maud together was probably their mutual passionate love of the stage. She had persuaded him to give her parts and, though the critics were sometimes unkind, she also had successes. In 1894 they crossed the Atlantic for a tour of America and Maud said the short time they spent on board ship was the happiest period of her life because she had him to herself. Once they stepped ashore she was elbowed aside and Herbert was besieged by female fans. The pair were lionized, loaded with flowers, and presented to President Cleveland. But the most important event was the night they went to a new play by George du Maurier. Called *Trilby* it had in it the part of a lifetime for Herbert Tree – Svengali, the weird, hypnotic figure for which he would always be remembered. He returned to England with the manuscript of *Trilby* in his pocket.

Sir Herbert Beerbohm Tree playing Svengali

Critics were not always kind to Herbert and his flamboyant, emotional productions. But they raved about his performance as Svengali. His greatness lay in the fact that he had the ability to transform his whole personality and appearance for a part without resorting to heavy make-up. He approached every performance as though it was his first. It saved him from staleness, though there were drawbacks. No one knew quite what he was going to do and his performances were 'as variable as spring weather'. Strangely, though a great lover in private, he was never very successful in romantic parts on stage. His performance as *Hamlet* delivered in his slightly guttural voice brought the devastating remark from W. S. Gilbert: 'I never saw anything so funny in my life, yet it was not in the least bit vulgar.'

Herbert decided he would have his very own theatre to celebrate Queen Victoria's diamond jubilee in 1897. He went off to America again to raise funds and returned to build Her Majesty's, declared by everyone to be the most beautiful theatre in London. The opening was a *tour de force* of fashion and beauty. Herbert proudly showed off his vast reception room in the dome of the theatre, which was to be both the venue for lavish parties and his retreat in years to come. The second season at Her Majesty's was marked by a stupendous production of *Julius Caesar* which had London talking for a decade.

Offstage things were not so good. Her husband's constant philandering had stoked up Maud's jealousy, though it is possible that she had not discovered the existence of his second family. She was presented with a marvellous opportunity for revenge. A handsome young actor called Lewis Waller had joined the company and fallen desperately in love with her. They became involved in a passionate affair. Tree was furious. It was all very well for men to stray, they had strong sexual natures, but wives were not expected to do so. One day, while Waller and Maud were out for a drive, they were involved in a serious accident in which Maud broke her jaw. Her injury, which spoiled her beauty for a time, brought out the kindly side of Herbert's nature and he was sympathetic towards the whole business. The affair came to an end.

He began to drift away from his legal family and their elegant house in Sloane Square and made more and more frequent excuses to stay at the theatre where, up in the dome, he had fixed up a comfortable, book-lined flat with a bed concealed in the wall. He would have an open fire burning there and food brought in. It was very cosy.

For Edward VII's coronation in 1902 Herbert wanted to produce a play called *Ulysses* by Stephen Phillips, in which the curtain rises to show the goddess Pallas Athene on top of Mount Olympus. He planned to replace the goddess with Britannia, and his roving eye had already spotted the perfect girl for the part. Her name was Constance Collier. She was one of George Edwards's Gaiety Girls, tall, statuesque and very beautiful. He summoned her to an interview in his eyrie; Madeleine Bingham describes their meeting and subsequent relationship in her biography of Tree. Constance Collier was apparently terrified of meeting the great man and had put on her best hat, featuring a large green bird, for the occasion. As he talked to her he stroked the feathers continually, making her forget everything she was going to say. She felt sure she had not made a good impression and had lost the part so she went off and joined another company. Months later she was summoned again. Herbert stared at her as she entered and continued staring for some time without saying a word. Just as her nerve was about to give he asked, 'Where's that bird?' More silence. He stood looking at her for some time, fingering his chin. Once he said 'Yes' very thoughtfully. Finally he asked her if she had ever spoken blank verse. The poor girl, by now a bag of nerves, blurted out that she had not. Eventually he asked her to read, which she did, not very well. At least, he said, she had the profile for Britannia and she was engaged.

For the next two years she lived for the moments when she could be with him. He was cool and professional with her at rehearsals but afterwards would pick her up in his newly-acquired car, an open tourer, and drive her out into the country where they would walk through fields hand in hand, calling at farmhouses for ham and eggs when they were hungry. She became his constant companion.

Suddenly, in the autumn of 1903, Constance became engaged to Herbert's younger brother, Max, whom she had met on holiday in France. Perhaps it was an attempt to force Herbert to regularize their relationship, but anyhow the Beerbohms did not welcome her into the family circle and just as suddenly she went off and married an actor called L'Estrange.

Herbert did not pine. He had enjoyed his lighthearted, laughing Constance for two years. There were still plenty of other demands on his life. He had bought Walpole House by the Thames at Chiswick for Maud, who had stopped having hysterics about his other women and accepted what she could not change. The Trees still appeared together at all the grand, first night parties. When he received a knighthood, and a heartwarming flood of congratulations from his own profession, Maud basked in the reflected glory and thoroughly enjoyed being a ladyship. Then, of course, he had to devote himself to his second family, which was growing at an alarming rate. There were plenty of rumours circulating in theatrical circles regarding his mysterious journeys to Putney, but no open scandal.

He had become very whimsical. Some people thought he carried the whimsy too far. He could be talking about *King Lear* one minute and whether one should eat winkles with a pin the next. His famous absentmindedness was also becoming something of a pose, perhaps to deter those who asked too many questions.

His favourite form of escapism was to go off to the famous spa at Marienbad, take the health-giving waters and watch the fashionably-dressed women flirting under silk-fringed parasols. On one of these trips, however, he met his match. He became desperately involved with a beautiful dark-haired woman, whose name is not known. They made love under the pines. She gave him a book of her poems in one of which she spoke of wanting to sink with him in a flaming kiss through everlasting night, into a single soul. On the fly leaf she wrote, 'take this book – it is thine with all its moans and memories of love.' Her intensity smothered him.

She pursued him, sought him out, swooned with passion. It was all too much. For once he had not been able to call the tune. He crept out of his hotel in the early hours of the morning, took a carriage to the railway station and fled back to England!

He was in Marienbad when the First World War broke out and for a time thought he was going to be trapped there. The thought of war upset him deeply and he kept repeating, 'Wicked, wicked, wicked.' He detested the glorification of battle and prayed that one day man would regard war with the same horror as he did cannibalism.

Back at His Majesty's Theatre he responded to the challenge by putting on the most colourful, patriotic plays in his repertoire in an attempt to keep people's spirits high. His other contribution to the war effort was to become a father for the tenth time at the age of 64.

Perhaps it would not have happened if he had not gone to New York. Herbert loved New York. He called it an 'electric city' and he always felt on top of his form there. It was in response to numerous invitations that he went over to America, where he met Constance Collier again, became great friends with Chaplin and filmed *Macbeth*. He also played a successful season at the New Amsterdam Theatre in New York and at a theatrical supper one evening was introduced to a pretty young English actress called Muriel Ridley. She was, at 32, just one year older than his daughter, Viola. The old chemistry began to work and they were in love. Typically, in the middle of this affair, he suddenly became worried about his loved ones in England and, desperately homesick, decided he must go home. Muriel Ridley gave birth to his son, Paul Ridley Tree, and had to be content with a telegram of congratulations. Honour had to satisfied and he later met her for dinner to make arrangements for maintenance!

Keeping three separate families did not seem to affect his wizardry in the theatre and his wartime production of *Chu Chin Chow* is remembered to this day.

One weekend in June 1917 he decided to take a break and went to stay at Constance Collier's cottage on the Kent coast. She had invited him to use it whenever he liked. The cottage had an old winding staircase with a handrail that was broken in places. You could suddenly find yourself holding on to nothing. Coming downstairs in the dark one night he pitched headlong down the stairs. His leg was not broken, as he thought, but a ruptured tendon above the kneecap meant a minor operation was necessary. Maud sat at his bedside while he was convalescing and he received a stream of visitors. All he could think of was getting back to work. But on 2 July, while he was peeling a peach, his head fell forward and the knife dropped from his hand. At first the nurse thought he was asleep, but he had been killed by a blood clot. He left a bevy of women to mourn for him, but the reading of his will must have given them all a shock. Half his estate went to the mysterious Mrs Reed.

Chapter
Four

ROYAL LOVERS

François 1

Night after night in 16th-century Paris a tall figure would slip through a back gate of the royal palace and into the shadows. A single servant would accompany him on his wanderings through the narrow streets. They would arrive at some half-timbered house to be received with low bows and ushered inside. Throwing aside his cloak, François I, that most virile of French kings, was revealed out on his nocturnal prowl.

Not content with his adoring queen, his harem of wellborn French women, his official mistress, François could never resist the thrill of a secret assignation, a carefully concealed affair. He wandered the streets at night prepared to risk everything for the thrill of making love to a pretty woman.

Yet François I, for all his philandering, was a great prince as well as a great lover. He towered above his contemporaries both physically and otherwise. He was a Valois, six feet tall, high-spirited with a magnificent presence and powerful body. His face was not classically handsome, pale, with rather curious almond-shaped eyes, a long nose and thick lips. But his looks were enhanced by a pleasing voice and smooth chestnut hair worn close into the nape of his neck like a page. His clothes were always splendid, strewn with pearls and diamonds, fastened with gold buttons and buckles. His shirts were kept in a case of scented Russian leather and the scabbard of his sword was jewel-encrusted white velvet. Everything about him, it was said, flashed and sparkled.

François was above all a man of action, happiest when riding to hounds, tilting at the joust or making love. Stories about his love of women were being circulated with relish even in his lifetime – they grew to legendary proportions after his death. One report sent back to the English court, said, 'The King is a great womanizer, and readily breaks into others' gardens and drinks at many sources.' It was alleged that he had a mistress at the age of ten, that he had incestuous relations with his sister and that he built the great château at Chambord simply to be near a woman he desired. There is certainly evidence that at the time of his accession he was having an affair with the wife of an eminent Parisian barrister, and even Mary Tudor complained that he had been 'importunate with me on diverse matters not to my honour'. Successive generations have not been able to resist adding their own stories until the only thing left was to turn him into fiction. He became the royal lecher in Victor Hugo's *Le Roi S'Amuse* and the Duke of Mantua in Verdi's *Rigoletto*.

Though undoubtedly he usually thought first of satisfying his sensual appetite, he also loved women as works of art, considering them an integral part of the decoration of his great palaces. He liked to see them beautifully dressed and from time to time would order trunkfuls of magnificent gowns for his favourites so that they could grace his personal landscape. It was estimated once that he spent 300,000 gold crowns a year – a vast amount – on presents for women.

Historically, he transformed the cultural life of France and ushered in the Renaissance. 'After a long succession of dreary kings he burst forth like the sun,' says his English biographer, Desmond Seward. As supreme patron of the arts he had Leonardo da Vinci and Andrea del Sarto as court painters. Leonardo actually died in his arms. Benvenuto Cellini was his jeweller and he bought the works of Raphael and Michelangelo for his palaces. The library he put together became the Bibliothèque Nationale.

This astonishing king came from a line that had reigned from the tenth century. He was born in 1494 and brought up in the palatial château at Amboise, growing to be a wilful, high-spirited youth, spoiled by the adoration of his mother and sister. Fortunately, he also had great qualities of courage and intelligence. At 16 he jumped at the chance to become a courtier at the palace of Louis XII.

By this time he had already taken part in his first sexual adventures and after barely two years at court his mother was writing with great horror of a disease in her son's private parts. He had, apparently, contracted syphilis in the arms of a generous lady called La Belle Ferronière. He was completely cured and warned to be more careful in future.

King Louis was childless so François, as senior prince of the royal blood, was heir presumptive. He was made Duc de Valois and given several magnificent royal residences. He was the hero of the young nobility who despised King Louis' meanness and frugality. They applauded wildly when François rode out to tournaments resplendent in cloth of silver, cloth of gold and crimson velvet, and crowed with delight over his nocturnal escapades.

Louis died on New Year's Day 1515 and the coronation of François I that followed dazzled the world. From this time on, whatever happened in his private life, François never forgot the mystic grandeur of the ceremony that made him King, never forgot that in some strange way he *was* France.

When the time came for him to marry, his bride was Claude, Duchess of Brittany in her own right. She was nothing like the King's ideal woman. Though renowned for her sweetness and kind nature, she was very small, dumpy, and walked with a pronounced limp. At first he took very little interest in her save as the mother of his children. Over a period of nine years she bore him three sons and four daughters. But the charm of her manner made her popular with everyone and François grew very fond of her. She adored him, bearing his infidelities with resignation. Unfortunately her life was short, no doubt due to such intensive childbearing, but when she died at Blois on 26 July 1524, he felt pangs of regret and said that if he could bring her back by giving his own life, he would gladly do so.

The King's favourite mistress in the year he came to the throne was 17-year-old Jeanne de Coq, wife of an eminent Paris lawyer, Maître Disomme. By all reports she had a lovely face, skin like a peach and a perfect figure. But Maître Disomme was elderly, had a vile temper and was fiercely jealous. The King had to be very discreet. He usually entered the lawyer's house through the garden of a neighbouring monastery, sometimes being forced into Matins by encounter with the monks. They thought him a very devout young man. On one occasion he was caught by the astonished lawyer. What on earth was the King doing in his house at that time of night? François hastily explained that he had long wanted to make the acquaintance of such a distinguished man but, his days being so full, he was forced to come at this hour!

Quite early in his reign, François, a fine soldier, twice led his army into war. At the historic battle of Marignano, when he astonished Europe by giving the Swiss their first real beating and recovered Milan for the French, he made his entry into the Italian city 'wonderfully fine and triumphant, sword in hand, clad in blue velvet sewn with gold fleurs de lis'. Marignano was instantly recognized as one of the great victories of French history and a medal was struck showing him in profile, wearing a plumed hat and looking younger than his 22 years. After Marignano François was, for a time, the most admired ruler in Christendom.

Over on the other side of the Channel, another young hotblood, Henry VIII of England, had been closely watching his rival. Henry, too, was in his prime. And he was eaten with curiosity. He had heard François was a great lover. Could he possibly be a great warrior too? When Henry first heard of the victory at Marignano, he refused to believe it. He asked French diplomats endless questions about François. Was he really as amorous as they said he was? Were his legs shapely? How much did he spend on clothes?

Early in 1518 François had acquired the first of his great official mistresses – Françoise de Foix, Comtesse de Chateaubriant. Now about 23, she was a handsome, dark woman with a forceful personality, both demanding and promiscuous. The relationship between them was one long saga of jealousy and reconciliation. Françoise infuriated the King by flirting with his great friend, Bonnivet, Grand Admiral of France, and by hinting how much she enjoyed the Admiral's company. Once, on his own way to sleep with her, the King almost caught her in bed with him. Bonnivet just had time to hide in the fireplace which, as it was summer, was filled with greenery. François unwittingly got his revenge by relieving himself in the fireplace and drenching his rival.

Francois I

The affair did not stop him from sleeping with other women. A modern biographer has written, 'He was as amorous as a cat, amorous and inconstant.' His favourites were members of 'La Petite Bande', a group carefully selected for their beauty and charm. Among them was the delightful Madame de Canaples, whose portrait hangs in the Scottish National Gallery. Like most of the women François admired, she was a brunette with a pretty, rounded figure and sparkling eyes.

His nocturnal wanderings often got him into hot water. One time when he was 'madly in love' with a lady of the court, he made his way to her bedroom only to find her husband waiting with a sword, obviously prepared to kill him. François very cleverly turned the tables by pointing his own sword at the wretched husband's throat and, commanding him to do the lady no harm, added that if he as much as moved, the King would have no alternative but to kill him. François then coolly sent the husband off into the night and climbed into his bed.

Restless by nature, François seldom stayed in any one place for more than three months. Moving the French court about was like moving an army, but he never counted the cost. When he rode from one place to another, as many as 18,000 people followed him, 12,000 on horseback.

He was by nature extravagant, and in the spring of 1520 he had a chance to show off as he had never shown off before. Henry of England was coming to France to see him, a visit that had been strongly advised when their two countries signed the Treaty of 1518. Hearing that François had grown a beard, Henry swore he would not shave until they met. The contest had begun.

The site of this historic meeting, for ever after known as 'The Field of Cloth of Gold' was in a valley known as the Val Doré, about six miles from Calais. Henry landed at Calais, at that time British soil, with Queen Catherine and a retinue numbering 5,000. François was waiting with 5,000 courtiers and nearly 5,000 horse.

Their camps vied with each other in fabulous splendour. The French King's own pavilion was almost 60 feet high, supported by huge masts and hung with cloth of gold, striped with blue velvet and sewn with gold fleurs de lis. Inside, the pavilion was lined with blue velvet, the ceiling fringed with gold. It was divided into rooms, some of which were hung with black velvet to show off the royal silver and crystal. There were four hundred similar, smaller tents – 'an entire town of silver and gold, silk and velvet and floating tapestries, shining in the sun'. Henry, determined to outdo his rival, erected a castle of wood and canvas, hung with green and white silk, Henry's personal colours, and with cloth of gold and silver.

It was a full week before the kings met, in the late afternoon of Thursday 7 June, the Feast of Corpus Christi. François was a magnificent sight. His doublet was cloth of silver, slashed with gold and embroidered with diamonds, pearls, rubies and emeralds. Over this he wore a cloak of gold satin shot with purple, round his neck the plain gold collar of St Michel. His long boots were soft, white leather, his hat black-plumed and sparkling with jewels. Henry matched his magnificence, wearing the jewelled Order of the Garter round his neck. They galloped towards each other at the agreed signal and after a period of great nervousness and doffing of hats, still in the saddle, they embraced each other heartily.

For a fortnight there was jousting and carousing and great feasting, then the exchange of rich presents and a Pontifical High Mass celebrated by Cardinal Wolsey. Their meeting on the Field of Cloth of Gold had little lasting effect politically but François and Henry formed a genuine regard for each other which they never quite lost. Years later, when François heard that the English king was dead he had a mass said for his soul.

François made his court a centre of learning and art, persuading the aged Leonardo da Vinci to come to France and bring with him some of his greatest paintings including the *Mona Lisa* and the *Virgin of the Rocks*. Desmond Seward in his life of the great prince describes the full Renaissance glory of his background. The floors of his châteaux and palaces were of marble or parquet and strewn with fine carpets instead of rushes. His tables were covered with cloths of gold, rich plate being flanked by Venetian glass, dishes of majolica and enamel, cups, bowls and ewers of agate and crystal, lapis lazuli and amber, sardonyx and jade. Rooms hung with rich tapestries were lit by flaming torches in burnished gold or silver sconces, by candles in crystal holders and by scented logs of juniper, apple and pear burning in great hearths.

Against this background, François arranged his collection of beautiful women in their rich silks and satins, glowing in Renaissance colours. But the French people began to count the cost of having such a flamboyant, spendthrift king. It took a decade to pay for the Field of Cloth of Gold alone. In the 1520s everything seemed to go wrong for him. Soon after his meeting with Henry, Charles V of Spain, the Holy Roman Emperor, was to challenge him, beginning a rivalry that was to last all his life. There were private griefs, including the death of Queen Claude. Then at the battle of Pavia on 24 February 1524 the glorious François was captured and humiliated by the Spaniards. Less than two hours after they had started fighting, 8,000 Frenchmen and their mercenaries had been killed. François, unhorsed, fought by himself, swinging a great gold-hilted sword, until he was eventually forced to surrender. Surrender also meant that he was the prisoner of Charles V, now the most powerful man in Europe.

The captured King wrote courteous letters to the Emperor, which were ignored. However, his entry into Madrid was almost a march of triumph. Dressed in his usual splendour and riding a magnificent horse, he was received with wild enthusiasm. The Spaniards were impressed by their prisoner. Some of the ladies, who it appeared particularly admired his legs, visited him every day, bringing flowers and gifts.

So lulled was he by this reception that he actually had the nerve to ask for the hand of the Emperor's sister in marriage, but it was refused. A rude shock awaited him in Madrid after all the flattering processions; Charles ordered his imprisonment in the tower of the Alcazar.

He almost died of fever, then of humiliation as one by one he gave in to Charles' terms for his freedom. He was to give up Burgundy, Flanders and Artois and he had to abandon his claims on Naples and Milan. He was told he could return to France provided his two elder sons were sent as hostages. Surprisingly the Emperor then said he would give him his sister, Eleanor, as his bride. François solemnly kissed her on the mouth to seal their betrothal.

On 15 March 1526 François crossed the frontier into France to be greeted with great joy. 'Now I am King again,' he cried out. He spent several months travelling in a leisurely fashion through south west and central France, showing himself to his people. It was probably about this time that he met Anne d'Heilly who was to take the place of Françoise de Foix.

He felt he needed a new woman in his life. Claude was dead, he was tired of Françoise, he had been forced to be celibate in Spain and he was in no hurry to tie the marriage knot with Eleanor. Anne, he learned, was the daughter of Guillaume d'Heilly, Seigneur de Pisseleu, a nobleman from Picardy who had married three times and had 30 children. She was only 18, maid of honour to Louise of Savoy, and he was enchanted by her cool blonde elegance and her sensitive appreciation of the arts. Within the year the King had added her to his 'Petite Bande'.

Françoise de Chateaubriant was at home in Normandy when she heard of the King's release and his return to court with a new mistress. Françoise hurried to Paris where she sought out Anne d'Heilly and among other things called her a 'fuzzy chit'. Hearing of her jealous rage and her attacks on Anne, the King lost his royal gallantry and called his former beloved a 'rabid beast'. He ordered her to leave court and retire to her husband's estates.

Anne asked the King to take back all the gold ornaments he had given his former mistress as they were engraved with words of undying love. But on receiving the King's messenger Françoise sent all her gold jewellery to be melted down and returned them as ingots. The King was impressed. 'Return them all to her,' he ordered. 'She has shown more courage and spirit than I would have expected from a woman in her position.'

After the death of Louise of Savoy in 1531 Anne became governess to the King's daughters, Madeleine and Marguerite, as a pretext to have her near him. He married her off to Jean de Brosse, Seigneur de Penthievre, three years later and made the willing cuckold Duc d'Etampes in order to provide Anne with a title. Eleanor had arrived to claim François as her husband but only duty and politics made him take her to his bed. Tall, with a long, sallow face, she was not unpleasant to look at but while only in her early thirties, she seemed middle-aged, placid and colourless.

The shocked English ambassador reported that when Queen Eleanor made her ceremonial entry into Paris in 1531, the King and Anne d'Heilly sat in a window together, laughing and talking before thousands of people. Though he was still sometimes unfaithful, Anne was the woman he loved for the rest of his life. Like all great mistresses she held him by virtue of her intelligence, not only her sensual beauty. He was also amused by her vivacity though her wilfulness began to be resented after a time. When he built Fontainebleau, thought by many to be the finest house in Europe, Anne was given a magnificent bedroom next to his. He also provided her with magnificent châteaux at Etampes and Limours. She remained golden-haired and attractive but portraits also show her shrewd eyes and firm little mouth.

Since he was a child François had burnt the candle at both ends. Now 52, he continued to take violent exercise in the day and to sleep with his mistresses at night. But life was catching up with him. His last years had been plagued by trouble and he never got over the misery of losing Boulogne to the English. Like many others in his family, he was tubercular, and he sometimes suffered from old injuries sustained in war. His life was wearing out.

When François died in the early hours of 31 May 1547, the Marshal de Tavannes, a shrewd observer, said, 'Ladies more than years caused his death.' Strangely enough, just before he died he had dismissed Anne d'Heilly with a wave of his hand and she had fled from him in hysterics. Also, strangely, for one who was so promiscuous, he had once written a couplet with a diamond on a window at Chambord. Translated, it read: 'Woman is often fickle; Mad is he who trusts her.'

Charles II

O f all the English kings none could equal Charles II, the 'Merry Monarch', as a lover of staggering virility. He was the Don Juan of royalty, the supreme rake among rakes. His 17th century court was the most sexually promiscuous ever known and he led it with untiring vigour.

THE WORLD'S GREATEST LOVERS

The number of children born to Charles, apart from those he acknowledged, has never been known for certain but once when he was addressed pompously as the 'father of his people' Lord Rochester was heard to mutter, 'Of a good many of 'em.'

But he was also a witty, tolerant and kind man who treated all classes of society with the same amiability and courtesy. Even Dr Johnson, who was a stern moralist, found a good word to say for him, excusing his excesses 'because his complexion is of an amorous sort'. It has been said that he was one of the best loved and one of the worst kings England ever had.

Physically he must have been very impressive, though he had little personal vanity. Once, while his portrait was being painted, he asked the artist if the likeness was good. The artist assured him that it was. 'Then, odds fish,' he exclaimed, 'I must be an ugly fellow!' The King's features were large and heavy, his complexion dark, but the quizzical good humour on his face made him extremely attractive. He was tall, had a dominating voice and dressed magnificently in silk, velvet and great froths of snowy-white lace. Strangers found him formidable.

The trouble with Charles was that he enjoyed ease and luxury too much. His court was turned into something resembling a Turkish harem and he spent hours lolling around on cushions, flirting with his mistresses or strolling through his parks with his courtiers and a troop of the pretty little spaniel dogs to which he gave his name. He had great capacities, which he never used to the full. Science was his favourite topic and he enjoyed talking to scientists and attending meetings of the Royal Society. He also had a sympathetic love and understanding of the arts, of poetry, painting, sculpture and the theatre.

It was his love of the theatre that led him to the mistress most people associate with him – Nell Gwynne. To her, he owed a great deal of his popularity. For Nell was no pampered, greedy courtier, versed in etiquette and protocol and determined to get all she could from the liaison. Nell was a common cockney actress, a seller of oranges, a good-natured bawd who made Charles laugh and loved him faithfully as no other mistress had ever done. As long as he lived he treated her with an affectionate regard that was never given to some of his more aristocratic beauties.

His life had not always been soft, self-indulgent and amorous. His childhood was spent in the formal, austere court of his father, Charles I, a monarch who was utterly faithful to his devoted wife, Henrietta. Charles II could never have inherited his hotblooded instincts from them. He was only 12 when the civil troubles in England came to a head and his father signalled the opening of the Civil War by raising his standard over Nottingham Castle on 22 August 1642. For three years he was kept close to his father, riding through England in the wake of the Royalist army, seeing battle after battle fought between Roundheads and Cavaliers. Sometimes he hardly knew where his next meal was coming from. Sometimes he came near to death. When he reached 15, his father decided he must be sent to France and safety.

From 1646 until 1660 Charles lived in exile on the Continent. These were years of wandering and waiting for news, broken only by a few rash visits to England, one of which ended with Charles – who would otherwise have been king – hiding from Cromwell's men in the branches of what became known as 'The Boscobel Oak'. As an 18-year-old prince, he made one noble gesture that should be set against future failings. Hearing that his father's life was in the balance, he sent a Carte Blanche to Parliament. This document, still preserved, consisted of a sheet of blank paper with his seal and signature at the bottom, signifying that he was ready to do anything to save Charles I from his executioners.

At this stage he was by no means the debonair gallant of later fame. Tall, gangling, taciturn and heavy-browed, he was ill at ease among the brilliant French courtiers and so impoverished he could not afford his own carriage. But as the years went by he discovered his power over women and life improved. He became a past master in the art of seduction and wherever he went, during those years of exile, there was always a pretty woman, ready to hop into his bed. There is no precise information about the number of mistresses he had in France but at one stage the diarist Pepys remarked that Lady Byron must be his 17th and before he left the number had risen, in some estimates to 40! Charles liked his women to be sophisticated enough to enjoy his favours without demanding too much of his emotions. His favourite was Isabelle Angélique, Duchesse de Châtillon – his 'Bablon' as he called her – who was an enchanting companion without demanding fidelity.

On Oliver Cromwell's death on 3 September 1658, England stirred uneasily and wondered what would happen next. Cromwell's son, Richard, was found to be totally inadequate for the role of Lord Protector and people feared anarchy in the unstable conditions that developed. It was decided to call King Charles home to restore the monarchy.

Flags flying, a squadron of ships set out from England to fetch him. Charles had taken up residence at The Hague in order to be ready. His condition was so desperate that it was reckoned the value of what he stood up in, added to the cost of his servants' clothes, was not more than £2. He was given an immediate allowance of £50,000 so that he could return to his kingdom in style.

As he set foot on English soil again, no longer a fugitive, on 26 May 1660, church bells rang out and people danced in the street. London had never seen such scenes of joy and celebration as this restoration of the monarchy after years of puritan gloom.

After King Charles had listened to hours of speechmaking he retired

Charles II

thankfully to bed where the luscious Barbara Palmer was waiting for him. Formerly Barbara Villiers, daughter of Lord Grandison, she was a dark-haired tempestuous beauty whose sexual prowess was to keep him enslaved for nearly ten years.

They first met at his court in exile at Bruges, just before the Restoration. Her husband, Roger Palmer, was a minor diplomat with strong royalist sympathies and she accompanied him when he went to the Continent to swear loyalty. Charles found her a fascinating creature. She had already been mistress of the notorious rake Lord Chesterfield, a fact which made him madly jealous, and had acquired a taste for wealth, luxury and jewels, which poor Roger Palmer could not hope to satisfy.

During the time she was his mistress Barbara exercised incredible power over the King. She could behave like a fishwife when thwarted and subjected the rest of the court to her imperious will and bad temper. But he would hear no evil of her. In the end, he tired of her demanding ways and her greed but when he first returned to England she flourished and Samuel Pepys, who was hypnotized by her beauty, confessed to his diary that when he went to bed at night he dreamed that Barbara Palmer was there and he fell asleep in her arms.

Though Charles would have been happy enough to spend his days dallying with his mistress and other beauties of the court, it was soon made clear to him that he must choose a queen. During his exile many princesses had been approached as possible partners, but they had not been eager to ally themselves with a penniless king without a throne. He had been humiliated several times. Now, he was in a position to choose.

After some deliberation, he plumped for Catherine de Braganza, Infanta of Portugal, a young lady whose dowry included Bombay, Tangiers and a vast amount of money. She was totally different to the sort of women Charles was used to, though pleasant in appearance with an affectionate nature. She did her best to please him. Only pregnancy kept the seething Barbara from coming to court and establishing her supremacy. Queen Catherine had been warned about the King's mistress before she left home. She knew well enough that Barbara dominated Charles, was the proud mother of one royal bastard and at that very moment expecting another.

Everybody dreaded Barbara's return to court The King, hoping to mollify her, gave the much cuckolded Roger Palmer a title, so that she could call herself Lady Castlemaine. Actually, after four months of playing the devoted husband Charles was ready to welcome his mistress back to bed with open arms. So glad was he, in fact, to see her that he committed an act of quite appalling insensitivity.

Knowing full well that his Queen dreaded even the thought of meeting Lady Castlemaine, Charles insisted that his mistress be appointed to the Queen's bedchamber. Catherine protested, but Charles would not listen to her. One day he led Barbara into the Queen's presence and begged to be allowed to present her. The Queen did not know who she was. When her courtiers began sniggering, however, she realized she was holding the hand of the dreaded Lady Castlemaine and fell, fainting, to the ground.

Even this appalling behaviour did not kill Catherine's love for Charles. She knew now that she could never change him and taught herself to accept his amorous, wayward nature. Realizing that she had to put up with Lady Castlemaine, whether she liked it or not, she made the best of things and to the relief of everyone approached her in a friendly manner.

Queen Catherine's deepest grief was that she could not give this fertile king a single child, whereas Lady Castlemaine had three sons and two daughters eventually recognized by their royal father. Statesmen pleaded with Charles to divorce Catherine and marry someone who could give him an heir. But he would not. Whatever his faults, after the bedchamber disaster he always insisted on her dignities as Queen and gave her what affection he could. When Lady Castlemaine insulted her once, he turned on her in anger.

Nothing, however, was permitted to interfere with the royal pursuit of pleasure. Love, to Charles, was an absorbing game in which his emotions took second place to his powerful sexual urge. He seemed to have no conscience, nor did he feel any moral need to curb his desires. His court, brilliant though it was, became increasingly decadent. The King in his maturity was exceptionally attractive and none of his women, and there were many besides his official mistress, could be angry with him for long after they had been discarded. He would be sure to make them laugh and could always manage to laugh at himself.

Queen Catherine had ceased to complain about them. She was discreet and rarely visited the King's bedroom uninvited. A delightful story is told about one occasion when she broke the rule and surprised him. Laughing when she discovered an embroidered silk slipper by the side of the bed, she then withdrew at once so that 'the pretty fool' could come out of hiding.

Charles began to tire of Lady Castlemaine. Their relationship was by no means over but her temper, her greed and her volatile personality were beginning to get on his nerves. Fate sent him a delightful antidote in the shape of his distant cousin, Frances Stuart. As soon as he saw her he was bowled over. Tall, slender, graceful, with a classic profile and a soft, sweet voice, she was also virginal and determined to remain so. Pepys tells how 'besotted' Charles was with his pretty cousin, how he would manoeuvre her into corners and kiss her in full view of the court. But that was as far as he was allowed to go. He did everything he could to win her, organizing balls and fêtes in her honour and writing poetry in praise of her virtues. But though he was terribly in love, for once he had encountered a woman who could withstand his amorous onslaught.

Nell Gwynne

She had no intention of climbing into the royal bed. Charles had her beauty immortalized by the goldsmith Jan Roettiers and for three centuries the coinage of Britain bore her profile in the image of Britannia.

Then, suddenly, 'La Belle Stuart' eloped with the somewhat unprepossessing Duke of Richmond. The court was shaken by the King's fury. He swore he would never speak to either of them again. But when the Duchess became the victim of smallpox Charles could not bear to think of her being ill and sent his own physician to attend her. She recovered and begged his forgiveness for any hurt she had caused him. Eventually he accepted both the Richmonds back at court; some said Frances then granted him favours she had denied him before.

Lady Castlemaine did not remain in favour for very long after this. Her eclipse came in 1667, very soon after that of Clarendon, England's great Lord Chancellor, whose downfall she had schemed for and gloried in. She found herself paid off with an estate and the title Duchess of Cleveland. Knowing full well that her star had set, she wisely decided to cross the Channel and live in France.

The King had widened his amorous circle to include ladies of the acting profession. One was Moll Davis, who claimed she was a bastard of the great Howard family, the other, Nell Gwynne.

Nell had no pretensions to grandeur; she was a cockney born and bred. Brought up in a tavern in the rough area around Covent Garden, she first worked as a barmaid, before moving up the social scale to sell oranges to patrons of the London theatre. She first appeared on stage as a comedy actress at the age of 17 when she became the mistress of Lord Brockhurst, afterwards Earl of Dorset. It was while she was under his protection that the King saw her for the first time at the Theatre Royal, Drury Lane.

Charles could not resist her with her sweet, curly head, joyous laugh, cockney wit and wonderful good nature. At first Nell's visits to Whitehall were fleeting. Then, in the spring of 1670 a new play by Dryden, in which she was to take part had to be postponed because she was pregnant. The King admitted he was the father and she became his acknowledged mistress with apartments of her own and a title – the Duke of St Albans – for her son.

About this time another ravishing beauty captured him. The King first saw Louise de Kérouaille in the train of his sister Henrietta Maria when she came to England to negotiate the secret Treaty of Dover between him and Louis XIV. He thought her a frail and lovely creature, but she was only 16 and his sister refused to leave her in his tender care. Henrietta Maria died and King Louis sent Louise back to England. The official reason was that he wished to place her in Queen Catherine's household. But many suspected she had been sent as a spy.

When Louise de Kerouaille arrived in England she and Nell became great rivals for the king's love. Nell spared no one her wit. She had nicknames for nearly everyone at court, which highly amused the King. She noticed that Louise, though very beautiful, had a slight cast in one eye and promptly christened her 'Squintabella'.

Charles gave Nell a fine house in Pall Mall but the French enchantress was made Duchess of Portsmouth and given apartments in Whitehall. These apartments were the cause of a great deal of controversy. They were made so luxurious that, even in a court used to finery, people began to talk angrily of the vast amounts of money spent. But the frail Louise had Charles under her spell and soon proved herself as skilful at intrigue as she was in love.

To the end of his life she fascinated and cheated him more than any other woman. She aroused great feelings of resentment for many reasons. To start with, many people suspected that she was spying for the French king, others feared her Catholic influence on Charles, yet others felt that she was draining him financially. One day a carriage which people thought carried the Duchess of Portsmouth, was attacked by a crowd. But a merry, curly head popped out of the window. It was Nell Gwynne who called out, 'Good people, be civil. I am the protestant whore!'

Louise was also a snob, and although only the daughter of a minor nobleman, liked to claim kinship with the older and nobler families of France. When she went into deepest mourning for one supposed cousin Nell also put on black and said she was weeping for 'The Grand Cham of Tartary'. Nell took comparatively little from Charles compared with the fortunes extracted from him by his other mistresses. But she was always ready to help those in need and is known to have given money for prisoners in Whitecross Jail.

Both had to learn to share him with other women. One of these was Hortense Mancini, an Italian beauty, niece of the all-powerful Cardinal Mazarin. The King's passion for Hortense was intense but soon burned itself out. She was dark-haired, turbulent, fascinating, but she also had a wandering eye and this Charles could not tolerate. Her errant fancy wandered from him to the Prince of Monaco who was paying a visit to England and before she could protest her innocence, she was out of favour.

Charles, not yet 55 and seemingly in good health, was looking forward to discussing with Sir Christopher Wren plans for his new palace to be built at Winchester. Then on Sunday 2 February, 1665 he rose from his bed looking pale after a restless night. As the barber began to fix the linen for his shave, Charles had a 'violent fit of apoplexy'. He asked for the Queen directly he had recovered from his first attack. She was present when his condition worsened and was so overcome that she had to be helped back to her room. It was now, in his manner of dying, that one sees the best of Charles II.

Queen Catherine sent a message asking him to forgive her for any wrongs she had done him. 'Alas, poor woman,' was his reply. 'She begs my pardon? I beg hers with all my heart: take back to her that answer.' He apologized to his attendants for being 'such an unconscionable time a-dying' and bore with astonishing humour all the primitive attempts of his doctors to save him. His last words were a request to his brother James entreating him to be kind to the Duchess of Portsmouth and his children and, 'Let not poor Nelly starve.'

Edward VII

For most of his life, as he waited for a throne, Queen Victoria's son Bertie played with fire. His portly, bearded figure, Homburg tipped over one eye, cigar in mouth, was right at the centre of the follies and extravagance of an age. He moved in a social circle which was never far from scandal and became the lover of courtesans and actresses, titled women and professional beauties. Queen Victoria told him when he was Prince of Wales: 'If you ever become King you will find these friends *most* inconvenient.'

Albert Edward, Prince of Wales, later Edward VII, had wayward passions that shocked his mother to the core. She knew of Lillie Langtry, Sarah Bernhardt, Lady Brooke and a few others. But no one dare tell her about Moulin-Rouge dancer La Goulue who greeted him in Paris one night. 'Ullo, Wales, are you going to pay for my champagne?' and whose name was linked with his around all the Paris dinner tables.

Born on 9 November 1841, 'a fine, large boy', he was greeted with joy by Victoria who wanted to turn him into a replica of her upright and virtuous husband, Prince Albert. He had a miserable childhood dominated by tutors, constantly reminded of the need to apply himself, to seek for perfection and submit to duty. Prince Albert forgave his son for having only average intelligence but he could not forgive his lack of diligence and willpower.

When he was 19 Edward was sent to Curragh Camp, near Dublin, as part of his military training. His brother officers smuggled an actress called Nellie Clifton into his quarters and he 'yielded to temptation'. Later, when he was back in England, at Cambridge, rumours about the liaison reached the Prince Consort. Though he was ill from overwork, Albert hurried to confront his son. Edward was contrite and begged forgiveness, adding that the affair was over. While in Cambridge Prince Albert, his resistance already low, caught a chill. Within two weeks he developed typhoid fever and on 14 December 1861, he died at Windsor.

Despite the sorrow Edward showed at his father's deathbed, Victoria, in her heart, blamed him for what had happened. 'Oh, that boy,' she wrote. 'Much as I pity, I never can, or shall, look at him without a shudder'. When she got over the shock of Albert's death, however, she began to see that her son's grief was heartfelt.

Early marriage was planned for the Prince of Wales and in March 1863, when he was only 21, he wed the beautiful Danish Princess Alexandra. After a short

Edward and Alexandra

honeymoon they moved into Marlborough House, which was to be their London home. The Prince was deeply in love with his bride but it did not stop his career as one of the most prolific lovers of his time.

Victoria hailed her daughter-in-law as 'one of those sweet creatures who seem to come from the skies to help and bless poor mortals' and tried to exercise restraint on her son's behaviour. But Edward decided it was time he took over the leadership of society.

As his mother and her advisers had come to the conclusion that he was not to be trusted with affairs of state Edward based his life on the sporting and social calendar. In spring he visited Biarritz, in summer he went to a fashionable spa, in autumn he went to shoot in Norfolk and in winter he enjoyed the glitter and glamour of a London season.

He plunged headlong into the pursuit of pleasure. His companions were the idle rich. He turned Marlborough House into a meeting place for the fastest society set in London and became a devotee of baccarat parties that went on till dawn. He loved music halls, gambling and racing. He had a voracious appetite and smoked like a chimney.

Princess Alexandra did not care for this sort of life. She was home loving, like Queen Victoria, and found her satisfaction in her children. She was a warm, charming person, who in spite of her exquisite personal appearance was notoriously untidy and unpunctual. Edward's affairs hurt her sometimes but, incredible though it seems, they had a full and satisfying family life. Edward adored his children and they responded to him. He was determined that they would not be brought up as he had been and allowed them a great deal of freedom. The younger ones were even allowed to race toast fingers up and down the stripes on his trouser leg!

Their marriage survived a succession of scandals and constant gossip. He came near to disaster when he was subpoenaed as a witness in the Mordaunt divorce case and asked in open court if there had been any 'improper familiarity' or 'criminal act' between himself and the beautiful Harriet Mordaunt. There had not, the Prince declared, though it was noticed that the terms of the question allowed a certain latitutde in the answer. Society waited agog for his first appearance in public after the court case. The question was, did his wife believe him? In answer, Princess Alexandra put on her finest jewels, took her husband's arm and for weeks appeared with him at theatres and balls. Surprisingly, even Queen Victoria rallied to his support on this occasion.

Edward was very fond of the English weekend house party. Shrewd hostesses knew exactly who to invite and who to leave out. They would always include one of Edward's 'friends' so that he did not have to sleep alone at night. He would attend the races or join a shooting party during the day, eat a rich, twelve-course dinner then, puffing one of his enormous cigars, bid the company goodnight and

Lily Langtry, often known as 'the Jersey Lily'

'Good old Teddy', Edward VII in 1901, the year he became King

retire, knowing that a certain bedroom would be left discreetly unlocked.

Edward always had one long-term mistress as well as casual affairs. The most fascinating of these was Mrs Lily Langtry, always referred to as the Jersey Lily. She was a clergyman's daughter, brought up in the Channel Islands. Her great beauty took her from relative obscurity to dazzling fame. When she entered a ballroom in white satin and diamonds she almost brought the dancing to a stop as people twisted and craned to see her. She had a passion for fine clothes, and couturiers allowed her endless credit just so that she would be seen in their clothes. But after five years as a royal mistress the creditors began to close in on her. Edward was beginning to cool so she became an actress, gaining a whole new set of admirers, including Oscar Wilde. The Prince, after helping to establish her career, discreetly withdrew and their relationship came to an amicable end.

He had far more trouble with Frances, Lady Brooke, later Countess of Warwick. Edward was deeply infatuated with 'Daisy' Warwick and abandoned his usual caution. Pretty and sophisticated, she was an experienced woman whose name had been linked with others. Her husband had a passion for field sports which took him away from home most of the time, leaving her unusually free. Edward saw her often and everyone knew he was mad about her. Unfortunately, however, one of her previous lovers was Lord Charles Beresford, one of his close friends. Beresford had been unwise enough to finish their affair and return to his wife. Daisy was furious and when she learned in 1891 that Lady Beresford was pregnant she exploded with jealousy and wrote a vitriolic letter to her former lover. The letter came into the hands of Lady Beresford who threatened to publish it. Only the swiftest and firmest action by Edward saved them all from a disastrous scandal.

On 22 January 1901 Queen Victoria died at Osborne. On her deathbed she had embraced the sobbing Prince of Wales and her last word was said to have been 'Bertie'. At last he came into his own. For the whole of her reign Queen Victoria had treated the heir to the throne as an irresponsible playboy. He was not allowed to see state papers, not allowed to question her authority. Probably her attitude had increased his wilful pursuit of pleasure. People did not expect him to be a good king.

He surprised them all. Edward VII, who became known to his subjects as 'good old Teddy', took to his duties remarkably well, showed a keen interest in foreign affairs and swept away the cobwebs that had cluttered Victorian England. At home, he did a great deal to adapt the monarchy to a more symbolic role in the constitution and abroad he made England more popular than she had been for decades.

Just before he came to the throne Edward had found the perfect mistress. Her name was Mrs Alice Keppel. She was a young, attractive, quiet woman who made no demands on his time but was always there when she was wanted. She was comfortable but interesting, and, best of all, was accepted by Queen Alexandra who sometimes enjoyed her company. She could be relied upon to keep the King from being bored, something he dreaded, and without preaching persuaded him to modify the taste for rich food and drink, which was ruining his health.

Edward's reign was tragically short and signalled not only the end of an era but the end of the old way of life. After 1906 his health began to decline. On 6 May 1910 he had a series of heart attacks and his old friends were brought in one by one to say goodbye. Among them was Mrs Alice Keppel, his mistress. Queen Alexandra knew he would want to see her and had the greatness of spirit to forgive all that had gone before and grant his last wish.

Chapter
Five

LUSTY LADIES

Cleopatra

There is not a single portrait to show us what she really looked like. The nearest we can get to her is a profile on a coin. Yet, 2,000 years after her death, her name is still synonymous with temptation, seduction and love. She is one of the world's legendary women. Cleopatra.

She gave her love to only two men as far as we know. Both were giants. Both great heroes of Rome at the height of its power. One was Julius Caesar, the other Mark Antony. Both found her a bewitching woman, exotic, clever, dramatic in everything she did – and a superb lover.

Julius Caesar forgot his military and political strife in her arms and would probably have married her if he had not been assassinated. Mark Antony, a brave and fine soldier, laid his sword at her feet and in the end died with her.

She was eighteen when, in 51 BC, she ascended the throne of Egypt as Cleopatra VII and formally married her brother, Ptolemy XIII, who was only a boy of ten at the time. The Greek-speaking dynasty of the Ptolemies, to which she belonged, had been ruling the country since the death of Alexander the Great in 323 BC. She was fiercely proud of her royal heritage and determined to preserve it, determined to keep Egypt free from the domination of Rome.

Cleopatra had not a drop of Egyptian blood in her veins. From ancient writings we know that she was fine-boned and well-proportioned and that she was exquisitely perfumed with all the rare concoctions of the East. A copper coin from Alexandria shows a young woman with a long, graceful neck, fine, large eyes, a nose distinctly Semitic. The mouth appears to be large and beautifully formed. Being an Eastern Mediterranean type, she no doubt had black hair and pale olive skin. Plutarch wrote that, 'to know her was to be touched with an irresistible charm. Her form, coupled with the persuasiveness of her conversation and her delightful style of behaviour – all these produced a blend of magic . . . her voice was like a lyre.'

She had lived all her life in an atmosphere of intrigue, murder and corruption, so had learned to be cunning and ruthless herself. Before they had been married long, she and her brother, the King, were literally at war with each other, their armies confronting each other at Pelusium.

The historic meeting of Caesar and Cleopatra came about three years after she had ascended the throne at a crucial point in this family war. Caesar, returning to Rome after some bitter campaign which had wearied him, decided to stop at Alexandria, which loomed before him like a mirage with its cool fountains, gardens and flowers. Now, he thought, was as good a time as any to sort out these Egyptians. He knew Egypt could not be brought fully under Roman control until the Ptolemies stopped fighting each other.

First, he summoned Ptolemy and told him to disband his army, then he sent a message to Cleopatra asking her to come back from Pelusium and meet him so that they could talk. She wanted to meet this Caesar, wanted to state Egypt's case in her own words. Her problem was how to get back. Her brother's troops were still fully mobilized, blocking her way to Alexandria by land and sea. However, by some skilful manouevre she managed to slip away by ship under cover at night. At the entrance to Alexandria harbour she transferred to a small boat in which Apollodorus, her faithful Sicilian servant, waited.

Apollodorus rowed the boat to a quay just below the walls of the palace. The following morning he was seen carrying a rolled up carpet over his shoulder. Guards at the palace, who knew him, waved him on when he said he had a fine specimen to show Caesar. Admitted to the great man's presence, Apollodorus laid the rolled up carpet on the floor and untied the cord that bound it. To Caesar's astonishment the Queen of Egypt rolled out, an exquisite little figure who smoothed her dark hair, sprang to her feet and hailed him.

He saw before him a 21-year-old enchantress. She saw a tall, fair man in his fifties with shapely limbs, a strong, attractive face, his thinning hair combed carefully forward over the crown of his head. His authority assured her that this was indeed Julius Caesar, conqueror of half the world, the greatest soldier, some said, since the famous Alexander.

This time it was Cleopatra who conquered. Caesar was a renowned womanizer in Rome but this queen of the Nile, playful as a kitten one minute, wise as serpents the next, was unlike any woman he had known before. That night they became lovers. The whole ambience of this strange and ancient land seems to have had an effect on him, so that next day he wondered if he had been bewitched.

When the 13-year-old Ptolemy realized that Caesar and Cleopatra were lovers, he knew he had lost, that she would keep the throne and one day be queen in her own right. Finding them together on obviously intimate terms, he rushed to tell his companions that he had been betrayed. For a time, however, Caesar brought sister and brother together and they consented to live in separate wings of the palace and keep the peace.

Caesar lingered in Alexandria for four months under the spell of Cleopatra. She enchanted him by showing different aspects of her character each day. Besides demonstrating the art of Egyptian lovemaking, which was renowned in ancient times for its subtlety, she would no doubt also have demonstrated her grasp of politics, surprising in one so young. When she entertained him it was with an exotic luxury different from anything he had known in the Roman

Cleopatra and Caesar

world. On one occasion, wanting to show herself to the Egyptian people in company with the mighty Caesar, Cleopatra ordered a fleet of four hundred ships to accompany them on a journey down the Nile. They themselves sailed in the state barge with its decks designed as arcaded courts and leafy grottoes.

Caesar's infatuation with the Egyptian queen nearly cost him his life. As he was lulled into a delicious sense of ease and languor, his murder was being planned. The boy-king Ptolemy had secretly ordered his troops back from the East and they were surrounding the palace in Alexandria. Both he and Cleopatra were trapped.

Only the arrival of Roman legions on the eastern frontier saved them. Fierce fighting broke out and Caesar had to extricate himself from what became known as the Alexandrian War. In the end, the Egyptians were routed and the boy-king drowned in the Nile, but Caesar, always the statesman, had his body recovered and buried in ceremonial gold armour.

By now Caesar knew that Cleopatra was expecting his child. Before he returned to Rome he confirmed her right to be queen and arranged that her surviving 12-year-old brother should reign with her as Ptolemy XIV. The baby was born in late June or early July 47 BC and Cleopatra called him Ptolemy Caesar so that no one should forget his paternity, though he was generally known as Caesarion.

Great celebrations had been planned in Rome to celebrate the Alexandrian victory and to everyone's surprise Caesar sent for the Egyptian queen to attend them. Her arrival caused a considerable stir. Those who had expected to see a half-savage were astonished by her exquisite appearance. She would be fully made-up for such an occasion with antimony and lamp black applied to eyelids and eyebrows, ochre to lips and nails, and henna, creating an orange red colour rubbed into the palms of her hands and soles of the feet. Besides her brother, the King, and her child, she boasted an imposing, elaborately-dressed retinue.

Caesar installed her in a house on the right bank of the Tiber and made no attempt to conceal his passion for her. Though Cleopatra must have thought nothing stood in the way of her becoming his Queen Empress, there was one serious impediment. Caesar already had a wife, Calpurnia, and though divorces were two a penny in Rome, marriage to a foreigner was not considered to be a marriage at all. But such problems were rendered theoretical by Caesar's murder on 15 March, 44 BC.

When she heard the terrible news she must have realized the danger of her position. She had lost her lover, her ally, the man on whom the fulfilment of all her dreams for Egypt were based. She had been in Rome for one-and-a-half years. Now she slipped quietly away amid rumours that she had miscarried Caesar's second child.

Consul Mark Antony was now the most powerful man in Rome though he had played no part in the murder plot. His rise to power had been almost entirely due to his association with Caesar, but now he emerged as a magnificent figure in his own right. He was a great soldier, tall, muscled like a gladiator, with a handsome, bearded face and curly hair. His good looks made him attractive to women and he was an insatiable lover. But he also had a reputation for being a man's man and his troops worshipped him. His talk was often bluff and ribald, he had a taste for rowdy parties and drink. For all that, said Plutarch, there was a noble dignity about him.

The emergence of Antony did not worry Cleopatra. They had met before. When she was 14 he was the brilliant young soldier who helped to restore her father to the throne he had lost. He stayed in Alexandria for a short time, even then not unaware of the disturbing beauty of the young princess. Now it was to him she had to turn to secure her own throne.

Violent crises convulsed the Roman Empire after Caesar's death. Antony found himself in direct conflict with Octavian, Caesar's adopted son, who was determined to claim his heritage. A clash between the two men was inevitable, but for the time being they divided the Roman world between them and gave the impression of being friends.

Antony assumed control of all provinces on the far side of the Adriatic. Since Egypt was already protected by legions under his command, and since he already knew the Queen, he decided to make Alexandria the capital of his eastern empire. From there he would seek to defeat Octavian.

First, he felt it was his duty to carry on with Caesar's plans for a war against the troublesome Parthians. Egypt's position in such a war would be vital and he needed her money and material support. When he reached Tarsus he decided he could delay no longer and sent an intermediary to bring Cleopatra to him.

She was in no hurry to meet Antony. She knew about his voluptuous tastes, his vigorous sexual appetite, about his military glory and his courage. She also knew he was married to the beautiful Fulvia, a woman of force and power in her own right. But Cleopatra was equally conscious of her own ancient royal dignity, conscious also of the fact that to her servants she was a goddess, Isis incarnate. She would meet him, but on her own terms, in her own time. So it was only after a suitable delay, designed to show that she was not at Antony's beck and call, that she set off for Tarsus.

Her arrival at the ancient port was never to be forgotten by those who saw it. Shakespeare, hundreds of years later, wrote: 'The barge she sat in like a burnished throne, Burn'd on the water . . .' and Plutarch, the ancient writer from whom he gleaned his knowledge, recorded: 'She came sailing up the river Cydnus in a barge with a poop of gold, its purple sails billowing in the wind, while her rowers caressed the water with oars of silver which dipped in time to the music of the flute accompanied by pipes and lutes. Cleopatra herself reclined beneath a canopy of gold dressed in the character of Aphrodite, the goddess of love . . . all the while an indescribably rich perfume exhaled from numerous censers and was wafted from the vessel to the river banks . . .'

The whole population of Tarsus flocked to the water's edge to gasp at the sight of the Queen of Egypt reclining under her golden canopy. Antony, waiting for her in the market place, expected her to come ashore, but she had no intention of doing anything of the kind. He waited in vain. When eventually he sent a messenger asking her to dine with him she declined and invited him to dine with her instead. Unable to hold out any longer, he accepted.

That night as the barge lay at anchor in the moonlit lagoon, Cleopatra proceeded to seduce Antony with all the skills she possessed. She was now 29 years old, at the peak of her physical and mental powers. Antony was fascinated from the start by her voice, her manner, her conversation. She led him to a banqueting hall below deck hung with purple tapestries, embroidered with gold. The whole room was brilliant with light reflected from a thousand mirrors, the air delicately scented, the tables set with goblets and plates of gold studded with precious stones. He was overwhelmed. Again and again he returned, his senses dazzled by this amazing woman. At another banquet she had the floor covered with roses to a depth of several feet and dissolved a precious pearl in a goblet of vinegar to win a wager with him. Consummate lover that she was, she adapted her tastes to his. While his sexual experience was vastly greater than hers she was versed in the exotic refinements of the East. By her intelligent assessment of his strengths and weaknesses she bound him to her.

He was a sensualist, like most Romans, and she knew that by enslaving him to his pleasures she could keep him by her side. He returned with her to Alexandria. Discovering Antony had a passion for gambling she played dice with him; aware of his love of wine, she drank with him and aware of his love of practical jokes, she would join him in escapades in the streets of Alexandria after nightfall. They walked in her scented gardens and for a whole winter delighted in each other's company. Then Antony came to with a start. In Plutarch's words, 'At last, like a man roused from sleep after a long debauch, he realized he must leave his mistress and look to his laurels.'

Everywhere, it seemed, Octavian had triumphed while Antony's eastern empire was tottering. From this moment on, his star began to wane. Fulvia, Antony's wife, had died while he had been dallying in Alexandria. He returned to Rome and, as an obviously political move, married Octavian's young and beautiful widowed sister, Octavia. The union was wildly popular in Rome for it seemed likely to avert civil war. But Cleopatra was filled with anger. Only a few weeks earlier she had given birth to Antony's twins. That Octavia was younger than she, and universally admired, only added to her fury.

Antony, however, could stand only so much of Octavia's virtue. She was a gentle paragon who lectured him about his drinking habits, his gambling and his health. He did not understand women like her. She suffocated him. Cleopatra was on his mind most of the time. She had understood his moods, joined him in his pleasures, laughed with him. Octavia had sailed with him on his return to the East, but when they reached Corfu, he sent her home. He knew well enough that the act would be construed as an insult by Octavian, that he was, in fact, throwing down the gauntlet, but by this time he was in the hands of destiny.

He sent a trusted friend to bring Cleopatra to him at Antioch in Syria. His 'betrayal' was forgotten or forgiven and they spent the whole of that winter together. The following spring he set out with his legions to march against Parthia. If the campaign had been successful his military glory would have outshone anything Octavian had done. But it was a disaster ending with the proud legions in a desperate state. Antony's judgement and timing had been tragically wrong and even his soldiers began to murmur about his obsession with Cleopatra.

In the early months of 33 BC it became increasingly clear that the 'alliance' between Octavian and Anthony would not last much longer. The whole Mediterranean stirred uneasily. And as war loomed on the horizon the names of Antony and Cleopatra were besmirched in Rome. He was, if anything, even more enslaved by her. At some banquet or other in Alexandria he was said to have risen from his couch to rub her feet with sweet oils, usually the duty of a slave. On many occasions as he sat in the tribunal he would receive love letters from her on tablets of onyx or crystal and would stop everything while he read them. Once, while Furnius, the foremost Roman orator, was pleading a case, Cleopatra passed through the marketplace on her gold litter. Antony leapt to his feet, left the trial and accompanied her, hanging on to the side of the litter, laughing, completely forgetful of his duty.

The fate of these legendary lovers was coming to a climax. In the year 31 BC Octavian declared war, using his strong fleet to seize Antony's eastern harbours and coastal fortresses one by one. Eventually he reached Actium, situated on the southern side of the Ambracian Gulf. Antony and his fleet arrived, anchored in the Gulf and Cleopatra joined him with her squadron of ships.

Octavian's plan was to stay offshore and lure Antony out to sea where his ships would be outflanked and outnumbered. For four months Antony refused to move. The sun poured down on the mosquito-ridden lagoon where he was trapped and conditions became intolerable. Disease was rampant and he was running out of supplies. On the second day of September, after advising Cleopatra to make for Alexandria, he decided to break out and the Battle of Actium began. Cleopatra's squadron, led by her flagship, the *Antonias*, moved swiftly through the two fleets locked in battle and made for the open sea.

Then Antony himself, in order to escape, transferred from his flagship to a lighter, faster vessel, caught up with Cleopatra and was taken on board her flagship. But while the queen went on to Alexandria, Antony and two companions dropped off at a small garrison town further up the coast. He had no intention of entering the Egyptian capital as a defeated man. News of Actium spread like wildfire and before long the eastern provinces went over to Octavian, leaving Antony with nothing but Cleopatra and Egypt.

Cleopatra knew that they were doomed. She begged Antony to join her in Alexandria and while he sat desolate in a tower on the harbour wall, she began collecting all the Ptolemy treasures under one roof.

Octavian was closing in on Egypt. She took all the most precious items of the royal treasure and also great quantities of firewood and tinder and had them stored in the mausoleum she had built for herself in the royal cemetery of the Ptolemies. Then, with her two maids, Charmian and Iras, she went inside and sealed the great doors.

Antony sent a message to his enemy offering to kill himself if he would spare Cleopatra, but he did not get an answer. Octavian's troops advanced steadily into Egypt until they reached the outskirts of Alexandria. There, Antony produced one last flourish of his military genius and forced them to retreat. But it was all over. His troops deserted him on land and his ships surrendered at sea.

At this moment of desperation a messenger arrived from Cleopatra. Her letter said either that she had killed herself or intended to do so. No one is certain which. At all events, believing Cleopatra dead, he took out his sword and asked his servant, Eros, to kill him. But Eros could not do it and turned the sword upon himself instead. Antony took another weapon and plunged it into his body, missing his heart.

When Cleopatra heard what had happened, and that he was still alive, she asked her servants to bring him to the mausoleum. As the great doors were sealed, Antony was bound to a stretcher and Cleopatra and her maids let down ropes from the window and gently drew him up. Cleopatra abandoned herself to grief, calling him her lord, her emperor, her husband. He died in her arms, beseeching her to make terms with Octavian for her own sake. 'Be happy with me,' he begged, 'in remembrance of the good times we shared in the past.'

When the victorious legions arrived in Alexandria, she was tricked into opening the door of the mausoleum. Octavian allowed her to have full charge of Antony's burial at which she grieved loudly and bitterly. But she knew what she must do.

On 12 August, she asked her guard to take a sealed letter to Octavian. It contained a request that she should be buried beside Antony. Octavian knew this meant she intended to kill herself. Guards were sent immediately to the palace, but it was too late. Cleopatra was lying on a golden couch dressed in her full regalia as Queen of Egypt. Iras lay dying at her feet, Charmian, also on the point of dying, was trying to adjust Cleopatra's headdress. But the Queen was dead. One of the guards cried out, 'Charmian, was this right?' Charmian's reply was a fitting epitaph for her mistress, 'It is entirely right,' she managed to say, 'and fitting for a queen descended from so many kings.'

Earlier that day the guards remembered a peasant had been stopped at the palace gate with a great basket on his arm. He took off the leaves that covered it and showed them that it contained figs, choice figs for Cleopatra. Beneath, unseen by the guards, lay coiled a snake, probably the very poisonous blackish Egyptian cobra thought to be a special protector of the Egyptian royal house. Two faint, barely visible punctures were found on Cleopatra's arm. The snake was never recovered though marks which could have been its trail were noticed on the beach beneath Cleopatra's window. Octavian followed her last wishes and she was buried by Antony's side with full honours.

Sarah Bernhardt

Men would fight duels for her. She was a siren whose affairs were the gossip of half Europe and who delighted in outrageous conduct as men like the Prince of Wales, Napoleon III and Victor Hugo fell on their knees before her. 'I have been one of the great lovers of my century,' Sarah Bernhardt told a close friend when she was old.

The legendary actress was not beautiful in a conventional way. Barely five feet in height, she had a mass of unruly red hair, an aquiline nose and closely set, intense blue eyes. But her body was sinuously erotic, her voice described as 'golden' and she exuded a femininity that was perfumed, exotic and magical.

Sarah loved to shock. In her bedroom she kept a coffin lined in rose-coloured silk. It travelled with her wherever she went. What did she do with it? Did she sleep in it, learn her lines in it, or, as scurrilous gossip hinted, did she lure her admirers into it for more intimate purposes? Stories about her affairs were so prolific that at one time the press distributed an astonishing pamphlet called 'The Loves of Sarah Bernhardt'.

For nearly 60 years her bizarre personal life and her magnetism as an actress held audiences captive all over the world. The 'divine Sarah' they called her.

Yet as a child she was tossed aside, neglected, ignored, told that she was ugly and that no man would ever love her.

Her mother, Judith van Hard, was a ravishingly beautiful Jewish courtesan who came from Holland. Her father, Edouard Bernhardt, was a law student. Sarah was born in Paris on 23 October 1844; shortly after her birth she was boarded with a peasant woman near Quimper in Brittany, and more or less forgotten. Appallingly neglected by her mother, she learned that the only way of getting attention was by creating a disturbance. Once she threw herself out of a window, breaking her arm, so that she would be noticed and listened to. After that, she was taken away from her nurse and sent to boarding school.

Only when she came into a legacy from her father was Sarah allowed to leave school and live with her mother in the elegant Paris apartment where Judith van Hard received her lovers and entertained the *demi-monde*. Sarah was well aware that her mother preferred her sister, Jeanne, who had inherited her looks and had been brought up in Paris with all the fuss and attention imaginable. Sarah, with her wild fits of temper and unruly hair, did not try to compete, instead producing disasters and crises at will in order to get her way.

When she reached 15 her mother suggested several suitors for Sarah's hand. The stubborn girl turned them all down. There was a family conference to decide what to do with her, to which her worldly Aunt Rosine brought her lover, the Duc de Morny. It was he who decided Sarah's destiny. 'Send her to the Conservatoire,' he suggested in an offhand manner, meaning the Conservatoire of the Comédie Française.

On the day she entered the Conservatoire her mother was too busy to go with her, as she should have done as Sarah was still a minor. Sarah decided she would have to make an impact on her own and arrived decked out in the height of fashion, in a carriage with footmen borrowed from Aunt Rosine. This did not go down at all well, either with her fellow students or with Thierry, the director. She hated the pompous, formal atmosphere of this theatre from the start. When she was eventually given a contract she felt no pleasure, only resentment that it was through the influence of the Duc.

To celebrate her entry to the Comédie Française Aunt Rosine gave a dinner party. The Duc de Morny brought with him an elegant young hussar, the Comte de Keratry. He did not take his eyes off Sarah, paid her many compliments and invited her to recite at his mother's house. He probably became the first of that long procession of lovers winding through her life. Now, even her mother could not deny that she had a certain magnetism.

Her first months at the Comédie were sheer nightmare. She was badly affected by stagefright and received with faint praise by the critics. She struggled on but found herself frustrated by lack of parts and in the end, after a row with a powerful older actress, walked out. She obtained a new position at the

'Gymnase' theatre, but in 1864, at the age of 20, had to leave. She told everyone nonchalantly that she was off to Spain where she hoped to marry a matador. The fact was, she was pregnant and did not want the whole of Paris to know.

Sarah had become the mistress of Henri, Prince de Ligne, who came from one of the oldest and noblest families in Belgium. They met in 1862 and carried on a discreet but passionate affair. Just before Christmas 1864 she gave birth to his son, her only child, Maurice. The Prince gave her a choice: either to marry him or to return to the stage. There could be no compromise. The choice caused her great anguish but she already knew that she had a certain genius that must be fulfilled and she chose her profession.

After the birth of Maurice, life was not easy. She accepted any stage work offered to her and for the only time in her life took lovers for profit rather than for pleasure. Finally she succeeded in getting an engagement at the Théâtre de l'Odéon. She was charmed by the young and elegant director, Duquesnel, and settled down happily in what was to become her favourite theatre.

Now she radiated a vibrant energy and became the idol of the Bohemian world of Paris. Life sparkled at l'Odéon. It was so different from the stuffy, parochial atmosphere of the older theatre. Even rehearsals were fun. Prince Napoleon, the Emperor's cousin, better known as 'Plon Plon', came to rehearsals. He was gallant in his attitude to women, had impeccable manners and great appreciation of the arts. Most people were convinced that he became Sarah's lover, but she was discreet about it. She already had Pierre Berton waiting in the wings. He was one of the most handsome actors in France and madly in love with her. More than once she had refused his proposal of marriage, but their relationship lasted for over two years and afterwards he said that their days together had been like 'pages from immortality'.

Her great talent began to unfold. She played the first unqualified success of her career in period male clothes when she took the part of a young minstrel in François Coppée's *Le Passant*. The critics said she spoke the poetry so exquisitely it was like listening to the song of the nightingale. From this time on she appeared in triumph after triumph.

The outbreak of war with Prussia, bringing about the end of the Second Empire, put an end to the applause but brought out unexpected patriotic fervour in Sarah. She persuaded the management to turn l'Odéon into a military hospital and volunteered to take on the task of getting food and supplies for wounded troops from the new Prefect of Police. To her amazement the Prefect turned out to be none other than her dashing first lover, the Comte de Keratry. He was soon under her spell again. He not only put his full resources at her disposal but let her take his overcoat as a blanket, sent her ten barrels of wine, two of brandy, 30,000 eggs and hundreds of bags of tea and coffee. Sarah helped to nurse hundreds of soldiers during the siege of Paris and faced the greatest

Sarah Bernhardt

misery and suffering with compassion. The effect was to subdue the wilder side of her personality. Her fits of temper and temperament became rare.

After the war the role of Queen of Spain in Victor Hugo's *Ruy Blas* made her a star of the first magnitude. Sarcey, the great French critic, who could be so cruel, was in ecstacy. After the first night performance the crowd of admirers around her backstage made way for Hugo himself. Before she could say anything he had gone down on his knees in front of her. Raising her hands to his lips, he murmured, 'Thank you, thank you.' Sarah wrote in her memoirs: 'He was so fine that evening with his noble forehead which caught the light, his stubble of silver hair like a crop out in the moonlight, his laughing, shining eyes.' Obviously delighted with each other, most people presumed they became lovers.

But Victor Hugo was not a young man and he had a rival. Playing 'Ruy Blas' to her Queen of Spain was an incredibly handsome young actor who seemed to have been born for romantic roles. Jean Mounet Sully was 31, dark, bearded with brooding eyes and a seductive voice. His performance was electric. Sarah had never looked more beautiful, wearing a white satin dress with silver embroidery, a train of figured silk and a little silver filigree crown on top of her blazing hair. Together they created magic. As she played opposite her lover Sarcey noticed, 'She was all tender, languorous grace' and she spoke Hugo's most lyrical passages 'like a long caress'.

These were the great years. Sarah began to see herself as the new Renaissance woman and as a proper setting built herself a 'palazzo' at the intersection of the rue Fortuny and the avenue de Villiers in 1875. It was sumptuous, for she always loved luxury, and it was built without any consideration of how she would pay for it. The place was half-studio and half-mansion, for when she was not on stage she used her immense creative energy to produce works of art, all of which needed a home. Half-finished paintings and sculptures were stacked everywhere. The drawing room window was like something out of a cathedral. There were dozens of dainty silk chairs, velvet couches, exotic hangings and towering tropical plants. Then there was her taste for the macabre: a skull autographed by Victor Hugo and that coffin, always ready for use. Her home also had a collection of dogs, cats, monkeys, fish, tortoises and other beasts – there was hardly space to put a postage stamp.

Sarah made her debut in the English theatre in June 1869 and she was the sensation of the season at the Gaiety. English society loved her from the start and pardoned her eccentricity and her unreliability with regard to timekeeping. She did not disappoint those who expected something spectacular offstage. After a visit to a zoo she returned with a cheetah, six chameleons and a white wolfhound to add to her menagerie.

It was an agent called William Jarrett – she said he looked like King

Agamemnon and had the most beautiful silver white hair – who finally persuaded her to go to America and set the seal on a decade in which she became the most famous international actress ever known. She took America by storm with her performance as the dying consumptive Marguerite Gautier in *La Dame aux Camélias*, a role in which Garbo also triumphed. There were incredible scenes wherever she appeared. The role brought her dozens of offers of marriage and countless cures for TB.

It was at the peak of her radiant career that she fell in love as she had never done before. In September 1881, her sister Jeanne introduced her to Aristide Damala, the son of a wealthy Greek merchant. Damala had a colourful, if slightly dubious, background. Onetime adventurer and officer in the Greek cavalry, he had also served his country for a time as a diplomat. He was forced to resign because of his habits, his affairs and indiscretions. In Paris he had spent the last of his inheritance and involved himself in numerous intrigues. His oriental parties at which his guests took off their clothes and plunged naked into baths of champagne were notorious. Gambling and a taste for morphine were draining him of the last of the family fortune.

But Sarah put all this to the back of her mind when he called on her one morning. She found herself in the presence of a tall, dark, handsome man who had a strange effect on her. He told her of his ambition to be an actor and after hearing him read a part she agreed to take him into the company.

Sarah was intrigued not only by his looks and presence but by his apparent indifference to her charms, which she used on him with full force. She allowed him to play opposite her in a production of *Hernani*, a decision which made some of her friends wonder if infatuation had not warped her judgement. They took the play on tour to Vienna, St Petersburg, Warsaw, Genoa, Basle and Lausanne, Lyons and Trieste then, finally, Naples. By the time they reached Italy she was madly in love with him. The tables were turned this time. Usually Sarah called the tune and dictated the temperature of a relationship. She was both piqued and attracted by Damala's apparent aloofness. He alone of all the men she had known was not immediately conquered. But she made up her mind to marry him, and before the company left Italy they were engaged.

They dashed over to England where the formalities of two people of different nationalities getting married were kept to a minimum and at St Andrew's Church, Wells Street, London on 31 March 1882, Sarah Bernhardt became Madame Damala.

Audiences that had been fascinated to see her on stage with her lovers were now even more intrigued to watch her play roles with her husband. Ellen Terry said of her, 'No one plays a love scene better, but it is a picture of love that she gives, a strange, orchidaceous picture rather than a suggestion of ordinary human passion.'

THE WORLD'S GREATEST LOVERS

The marriage was a disaster. Damala continued to have affairs with other women and there were terrible scenes of jealousy. Professionally he was equally disastrous. Managements would not accept him as a leading actor and he became envious and bitter towards his famous wife, resenting her fame. Sarah did all she could to try to placate his injured pride, even to the extent of having a play written for him and leasing a theatre where he might be the undisputed star.

When they next appeared together Damala seemed to have improved and was given quite good reviews. For Sarah, however, it was another triumph. 'That electrical, chimercial woman had once again conquered Paris,' wrote critic Jules Lemaître. It was too much for Damala. After a terrible row in which he accused her of trying to wreck his stage career, he packed his bags and left the avenue de Villiers. By now he had become addicted to morphine.

She suffered greatly but carried on playing night after night in Sardou's *Fedora*. In February 1883 he suddenly returned to her but his physical condition had deteriorated. In an attempt to end his dependence on drugs she threw away all the morphine and syringes she could find. Almost beserk with rage, Damala stormed out of the house again and this time she obtained a legal separation.

After his departure Sarah sought consolation in the arms of a burly, bearded poet, Jean Richepin, who produced several expensive theatrical failures for her, but being handsome and adoring, he was forgiven. Richepin was involved in one of the most sensational scenes Sarah ever created offstage. A notorious book, *Mémoires de Sarah Barnum*, had been brought out by an actress called Marie Colombier who, Sarah realized, she must have slighted at some time. The book suggested that Sarah's rise to fame could be attributed to two things: publicity and sex. The young Maurice Bernhardt offered to defend his mother's honour by fighting a duel with anyone who would stand up in place of Marie Colombier. Fortunately, no one came forward. It was Sarah herself who settled the score. She headed for Colombier's apartment, taking Richepin with her. The actress, seeing La Bernhardt bearing down on her like a vengeful tornado, tried to hide behind a curtain. Sarah found her, hauled her out, and chased her through the house with a horsewhip, wrecking everything in sight as she went.

Philippe Garnier became her new leading man and, as she was always susceptible to handsome actors, he replaced Richepin in her arms. Actually, he had been there before. He was an old lover returned, a lover who had been displaced by Damala but who bore no grudge and was ready to worship her again. He played the Emperor Justinian to her Theodora in Sardou's play of that name. It was a production of Byzantine splendour. In one scene Sarah wore a dress of sky blue satin with a train four yards long, covered in embroidered peacocks with ruby eyes and feathers of emeralds and sapphires.

Late in April 1886, with Garnier by her side, she set out on one of her mammoth tours. She travelled with her own company in special trains and steamers, always the centre of attention with her lover in attendance, her favourite animals and mountains of luggage. As many as 80 trunks would be needed to contain all her dresses, hats, shoes, personal linen and jewellery. Edmond de Goncourt, the French writer, gave a picture of Sarah in those years at the height of her fame: 'She arrived in a pearl grey tunic, braided with gold. No diamonds except the handle of her lorgnette. A mothlike wisp of black lace on the burning bush of her hair; beneath, the black shadow of lashes and the clear blue of her eyes . . . she must be nearly 50. She wears no powder and her complexion is that of a young girl.' Sarah wore no powder but she drenched herself with an expensive perfume so penetrating that a man's sleeve, if she took his arm, smelt of it for hours afterwards.

Offstage she was generally kind and good-natured with a great sense of loyalty to members of her family and old friends. What has been described as 'her greatest act of love' came in May and June of 1889 when Damala, dying of morphine addiction, turned up for the last time. He was penniless, a ghost of his former self, and pleaded to be allowed to act with her once more. Overcome with pity, she agreed. For several weeks she performed *La Dame aux camélias* by his side. Half Paris came to see them, but it was tragically obvious that he was dying. When he could no longer carry on, she traced him to a dark, sparsely furnished room in which the only decorations were a sabre he had once worn on stage, a gold crown and a Greek flag. She had him taken to hospital, assuring the authorities she would pay all the bills.

Aristide Damala was buried in Athens. Visitors to Sarah's house always noticed, in a place of honour, a marble figure she had sculpted of her husband in one of their few happy moments together, lying nonchalantly on his back, his hands under his handsome head.

She made her greatest world tour in the years from 1891 to 1893, and when she reached 55 had the ultimate satisfaction for an actress of seeing her name above her own theatre. Life had taught her aristocratic tastes and behaviour. Even in summer weather she usually appeared muffled to the ears in chinchilla or sables. But the house in which she now lived on the boulevard Pereire betrayed the real Sarah Bernhardt who had to be almost smothered in possessions before she felt secure. Most people, if they were honest, found it pretty awful. It was stuffed with bric-à-brac and animals both dead and alive. Dame Nellie Melba, the great Australian singer, never forgot her first visit. 'There were heavy stuffs hanging everywhere,' she recalled, 'drooping down and catching the dust; skins of animals on the floor, heads of animals on the walls, horns of animals on the mantelpiece, stuffed tigers, stuffed bears, even a stuffed snake.' Swarms of Buddhas inhabited dark corners and there were Chinese curios, bronze statues and ivories. The walls and ceiling were hung with red cotton material adorned with Mexican sombreros, feather parasols, lances and daggers. Amidst all this tawdry splendour sat Sarah. Folding doors would be flung open to reveal an exquisitely dressed figure ready to receive her guests like a queen giving audience.

It was in 1905 that the tragic accident occured that was to affect the rest of her life. She was in Rio de Janeiro playing the name part in *Tosca*. The final scene required her to commit suicide by leaping to her death from a parapet. Mattresses were placed so that they would break her fall. One night someone forgot them. She fell heavily, taking the weight on her right knee, and fainted from the pain. The doctor called to attend to her had such dirty hands she refused to let him touch her. She insisted she would rather wait and see a specialist when they got to New York. That meant three weeks delay and the delay was disastrous. Though she carried on with her career as though nothing had happened, she was never to be free from pain again in spite of treatment with ether and morphine.

By 1914 she knew she had gangrene. She accepted the fact with typical courage and said to the doctors, 'Do what is necessary.'

They amputated her leg.

Even this did not mean the end of her career. She managed to invent dozens of clever little devices which enabled her to perform without revealing the extent of her disability. Still, in the final stages of her life, she gave a strange illusion of beauty. She invited the showman C.B. Cochran to tea with her in Paris and he said he had never passed a more wonderful hour. 'After five minutes I felt this woman was not old and crippled but beautiful and strong.' The siren could still mesmerise. One of the last friends she saw, Mrs Patrick Campbell, arrived for dinner and found Sarah resplendent in a gown of pink Venetian velvet. She explained with great satisfaction that it was a gift from an admirer – Sacha Guitry.

Sara continued working until nearly her last breath. In 1922 she announced she would appear as the clairvoyant in a film called *La Voyante*. But she was already suffering from uremic poisoning and as the poison spread through her body her glorious powers began to wane. She died on the evening of 26 March 1923. Her last request had been for spring flowers so they covered her pillow with white and purple lilac, violets and roses. Then, dressed in a white satin robe they laid her in the rosewood coffin lined with rose-coloured silk.

Pauline Borghese

Perhaps the hot, Corsican blood ran more strongly in her veins than in the rest of the family, but Napoleon's sister Pauline was a problem from the day she began to notice men. As one contemporary put it, she was a creature of 'bizarre moral habits'. Headstrong, wilful, beautiful and incredibly amorous, she became so exhausted by lovemaking during one affair, she had to be carried about on a litter!

All the same, she was Napoleon's favourite and he fondly called her 'Paulette'. Like him, she was intensely dramatic and the spoiled darling of the Bonaparte family. Born in Ajaccio, the capital of Corsica, just like her famous brother, she was only 15 when the family left and settled in Marseilles. Like most Corsican girls she matured early and was a great success in the social world at an age when most of her contemporaries were still at their books.

She had no education, no artistic talent, no dowry. Her sole asset at this stage was her beauty, and that was remarkable. Her small head was perfectly moulded, her face pure oval in shape with a clear, olive complexion. She had lovely hazel eyes and teeth like regular pearls. Her figure was superb and she knew it. The Duchesse D'Abrantes described her breasts as 'white as alabaster and seemingly ready to take flight from her corsage like birds out of a nest'. Canova, the famous sculptor, modelled the perfection of her form for the Villa Borghese. He was said to have adored her artistically, but most men adored her in quite another way.

She had scores of admirers among her brother's political supporters. One of the first to fall in love with her was Napoleon's aide de camp, dashing cavalry officer General Junot. He followed her everywhere, but as he had nothing but his army pay Napoleon refused to let him marry her.

Pauline's first serious affair happened when she was 16 with a man twice her age. Louis Stanislas Freron, with whom she fell hopelessly in love, was a violent revolutionary as well as a womanizer. He was said to wear rose-coloured breeches so tight that everyone wondered how, having got them on, he ever got them off. To such a worldly and practised seducer Pauline's freshness was enticing. She found it thrilling to be desired by a man of his distinction and notoriety. Besides, he was a godson of the King of Poland and the Bonapartes were always vulnerable when it came to titles.

Five months after their first meeting they were lovers. Madame Mère, her mother, forbade any further meetings when she heard what was going on.

137

Pauline refused to give him up. She wrote him long, passionate letters and only the combined efforts of the family kept them apart. Napoleon, thinking it would give her time to cool down, offered her a comfortable apartment in the Serbolloni Palace, which he had taken for his own use. Here, Napoleon's wife, Josephine, showed her every kindness. Pauline hated her. 'This Creole woman,' she spat out, had been the first to say she would disgrace herself by marrying Freron. For the rest of her life she treated Josephine with hostility for spoiling her love affair.

Pauline's daily life was a round of pleasure. Sometimes she behaved like a frivolous schoolgirl, playing tricks, mocking important people. Then Napoleon would give her one of his terrible glances which he used to cow the most formidable of men. But she would merely pout and carry on with her frivolity. She was an *enfant terrible* of the first order.

While in the social whirl of Paris at the age of 17, she ensnared the handsome General Leclerc, 'the only man I ever really loved' she said afterwards, though she said that about every man in her life. Napoleon was delighted. He had actually picked him out as a husband for her.

Leclerc was a curious man who copied Napoleon in every way, even trying to walk and talk like him, though he was as fair as Napoleon was dark. From the moment he saw Pauline, he adored her. Pauline shocked and hurt him, but they married and she gave him a son.

She was happy as long as they were in Paris, but to her horror Leclerc was posted to San Domingo in October 1801 and Napoleon gave specific orders that Pauline should accompany him. Wholly ignorant of geography, she imagined the island to be inhabited by cannibals and wild beasts. It was only when someone told her she would look charming in Creole costume that her temper cooled down. The truth was, Napoleon, growing disturbed by her amorous behaviour, wanted her out of Paris.

On 20 November she joined her husband at Brest to embark for San Domingo accompanied by a pyramid of trunks, boxes and suitcases. She was somewhat appeased on her arrival by a succession of balls and receptions in her honour. But the posting was ill-fated. Yellow fever swept the island, decimating the army Leclerc had taken out with him. Eventually the General himself was struck down. Pauline refused to leave him and nursed him with devotion. But he died and she became a widow. She had his body embalmed, Egyptian fashion, and laid a strand of her own hair across his forehead before the coffin was closed and shipped back with her to France.

Though she did not know it, she had also left behind in an unmarked grave another victim of the fever – her former lover, Freron. He had travelled out steerage on the same boat on which she was treated like a queen.

On her return she was a pitiful little figure after all she had been through, but she soon began to recover and fret under all the restrictions demanded by her mourning. Her only consolation was knowing that she looked marvellous in black. But what was the use of looking marvellous if there were no men to admire her? In spite of Napoleon's watchful eye she managed to devastate the bluff and rather stout Admiral Decres, who became a shadow of his former self through unrequited love.

When the mourning came to an end she burst upon the world again with a devastating display of her charms. At a fancy dress ball being given for Napoleon in Paris, she was met with gasps of astonishment as she triumphantly entered the ballroom dressed as a bacchante in a revealing, diaphanous white tunic embroidered in gold, her dark hair taken up with a band of tiger skin and grapes. In the splendour of her youth she was a vision. All the men applauded but the women called her dress 'une toilette effronte'.

Napoleon, secretly amused, decided he had better marry her off again to stop her scandalous behaviour. The man he suggested came from one of the greatest Italian families, so he felt that ought to please her. Prince Camillo Borghese was only 28, handsome and the richest man in Italy. But he was also utterly devoid of brains, a dandy who could not even write his own language properly. Pauline agreed to marry him. But he was to regret it.

They were married in 1803 and almost as soon as the wedding was over she started to plan how she could leave him. It was generally thought that Prince Camillo's fault lay in the fact that he was not a sexual athlete. Pauline already had a son by her first husband but Borghese did not seem able to oblige. She began to express herself volubly about the size of her husband's private parts and the insufficiency of his calves. In fact what actually happened was that for the next 12 years she waged what amounted to a terrorist war on the wretched man.

When Napoleon proclaimed himself Emperor on 18 May 1804, he made Pauline an Imperial Highness, which gave her precedence over her husband, a position she relished. Napoleon stopped her nonsense by making Borghese an Imperial Highness, too.

In Rome she assumed imperial airs and spent a fortune. Everyone was expected to wait for her as she could never be punctual. She would 'receive' guests at her morning toilette, chiefly to display the beauty of her dark hair. Visitors would be admitted to her boudoir to find her reclining before a mirror in a floating white négligée. When she started to take it off, it was a signal to depart, though some lingered longer than others. Every day she bathed in milk, twenty litres being delivered early in the morning for this purpose alone.

After a time she told the Prince she no longer wanted to live with him in the Borghese Palace, though it was big enough for them to be able to avoid each other for weeks. She said she must have houses and villas of her own. For the sake of peace, he gave her one at Frascati and another in Rome. But Pauline hated

THE WORLD'S GREATEST LOVERS

the rigidity of the Roman social scene and continually rebelled against it. Napoleon wrote to her sternly, warning her that he would never receive her without her husband. Eventually, however, worn out by her pestering, he agreed she could return to Paris.

The Prince gave up any further efforts to gain her love and with a sigh of relief, happily accepted the Order of the Golden Fleece from Napoleon and left Pauline to get on with her own life.

During the winter of 1805–6 she opened her salon at her fabulous house in the rue Saint Honoré. Her salon, with its yellow silk walls and crystal chandeliers, was the scene of the most glittering occasions in Paris. Of all the men jostling for her attention, she chose Jules de Canonville, a foppish man about town and one of Prince Wagram's aides de camp. They became lovers but Napoleon put a stop to the affair. For once he was really angry with her. He had, it so happened, just given her a present of a magnificent Russian cloak lined with sable. It had been presented to him by Tsar Alexander. The very next day, at a review, he was astonished to see the cloak thrown nonchalantly around the shoulders of Canonville. Within twenty-four hours the Colonel was ordered out of France to St Petersburg and when the Franco-Russian war broke out he was killed in action. Pauline threatened she would kill herself or go into a convent, but Napoleon eventually succeeded in calming her down. However Canonville had meant a great deal to her. She wore a miniature of him until the day she died.

Though devastated, she consoled herself with Auguste Duchard, a handsome young artillery officer, and with Talma, the actor, who was as romantic off stage as he was in performance.

Now she met the man who was destined to have considerable effect on her as a lover – Nicolas Philippe Auguste de Forbin. At this time about thirty years of age, a successful society painter from an illustrious family, he was a polished, elegant, splendid figure and extremely well endowed sexually. Women raved over him and Pauline, intrigued, made him her chief chamberlain. He took control of her household in a most competent way and broadened her intellectual horizons. And, of course, he became her lover. She bought a charming little villa in Nice so that she could enjoy a summer idyll with him, but with the end of the summer came the end of the affair.

Pauline was in a state of utter exhaustion and had to be carried about on a litter. No one dared tell Napoleon the reason but they did tell Madame Mère, who delivered a stern moral lecture and told her she must never see Forbin again. Pauline was so angry and in such a nervous state that for a few weeks any dog that barked within her hearing was shot forthwith.

Forbin prospered. When the Bourbons were restored to the throne of France, after Napoleon, he became director of the Louvre.

Between lovers Pauline played the hypochondriac, forever calling for cashmere shawls and hot water bottles. She spent much time lying languidly on her couch, complaining she was too weak to rise. But as soon as a possible lover came in sight her vanity forced her to her feet and to her interminable beauty routines.

She had begun to worry about her looks and took to wearing ten strands of pearls to conceal the slight wrinkling of her neck. She was as comically vain as ever. 'If you would like to see my feet,' she said to the Princess Ruspoli, 'come and visit me tomorrow morning.' The showing of the feet turned into an elaborate ceremony.

After Forbin's departure she appointed Felice Blangini as her director of music and took singing lessons from him, but it was soon obvious that she was more interested in finding out what he could teach her about love. Her last lover was Giovanni Pacini, a handsome young composer, chief rival to Rossini. She called him Nino, had his opera *The Slave of Bagdad* performed at her house, and hung on his every note. But for once in her life she had to face the fact that a man had lost interest in her before she was ready to declare the game over.

In spite of all her frivolity Pauline had one great loyalty and love throughout her life and that was for her brother Napoleon. She never let him down. When he was sent into exile she begged to be allowed to go with him. She offered to give him all her jewels if they would buy him comfort. When he was in the throes of his last illness she begged to be allowed to go and nurse him, but after he left the shores of France she never saw him again.

Pauline never got over the shock of his exile and death. In 1825, dangerously ill herself with cancer, desperately needing a friend, she asked her husband, Prince Borghese, to receive her at his palace in Florence. After some heartsearching, for he was perfectly happy as he was, he agreed. Though she had told him as long ago as 1812 that she wanted nothing more to do with him he treated her with great tenderness and she died in his arms.

Chapter
Six

PLAYBOYS

THE WORLD'S GREATEST LOVERS

Aly Khan

Aly Khan was a twentieth century Eastern prince who might have stepped from the pages of the Arabian Nights. Fortified by a potent brew of exotic mushrooms which, it was rumoured, he took every day, he devoted himself to the pursuit of women. Over three decades, until his death in a car crash in 1960, he earned a reputation as a great and tireless lover.

He had an electrifying effect on the female sex. Newspapers chronicled his affairs with relish, especially when they involved such famous actresses as Gene Tierney, Yvonne de Carlo, Kim Novak, Joan Fontaine and Rita Hayworth, whom he was reported to have snatched from under the nose of the Shah of Persia who was looking for a new wife. But they were only the tip of the iceberg. The tireless Aly had scores of other affairs, all of which he conducted with superb style. Elsa Maxwell, the famous party giver of the thirties, said shrewdly, 'When Aly falls in love with a woman, he falls madly and deeply. But she has to be prepared for the fact that his passion might last for only one night . . .' He lived entirely for the moment, hurtling round Europe in a red sports car, catching planes as other people catch buses – and always arranging that a beautiful woman would be waiting for him at the end of the journey.

Aly Khan's life reflected the clash of two worlds. In the West there was his everlasting pursuit of pleasure and passion. In the East there was his spiritual heritage. His father, the fabulously wealthy Aga Khan, was leader of the Ismaili sect of Moslems and, as his eldest son, Aly fully expected to take over from him when he died. But that leadership was to be denied him. It was the price he had to pay.

Watching him handle a difficult horse, or drive like a madman at the wheel of a car, no one would have guessed that Aly had been a weak, delicate child who had to be educated at home by tutors. His mother, whom he adored, was a beautiful Italian dancer who had been introduced to the Aga Khan in Monte Carlo and had gone through a form of Moslem marriage with him in 1908, a marriage which meant that she could be discarded at any time. Not until Aly was 11 were his parents united with full Moslem rites in Bombay. The little boy with soulful brown eyes hardly ever saw his awe-inspiring father, who led an international life, a great deal of it on the horseracing circuit. Aly said later that he could only be sure of meeting his father during the British flat racing season, and even then their brief encounters had to be fitted in between trainers and jockeys, politicians and Ismaili visitors.

When he reached teenage he was removed from his mother's influence and sent to England to be brought up as a European gentleman. His father made sure he found his way into the 'best houses', that he hunted with the exclusive Southdown and joined the right clubs. He provided Aly with a fully-furnished, fully-staffed London house, a generous allowance and plenty of tips about horses.

By the time he was 18, the young Prince with his sleek black hair, soft seductive dark eyes and silken manners had begun to make the other young men who attended Hunt Balls and London dinners look rather insipid. Any idea of university was forgotten. His tutors had found him to be extremely intelligent but unable to concentrate for very long. He was restless, volatile, courted danger – no one ever knew quite what he would do next. Aristocratic English girls were beginning to fall for him like skittles.

Hearing of the highlife his son was leading, the Aga Khan decided Aly must go in for a profession and arranged for him to study Law. He was in Chambers in Lincoln's Inn for a time but was never called to the Bar. 'Other distractions proved too great, and the Law, too dry . . .' noted his biographer, Leonard Slater. He rented a splendid house in Carlton House Terrace so that he could study in comfort and took another place in Warwickshire for weekend hunting. Books were put aside in favour of his other skills. It soon became obvious that no one could surpass Aly once he set out to captivate a girl.

His first major conquest was made in the corridors of Buckingham Palace. It was 1930 and London's loveliest and most exciting debutante was unquestionably Scottish-born Margaret Whigham, later to become Duchess of Argyll. That summer the dark-haired beauty with deep, compelling eyes was presented at Court according to the social custom of the day. As she left the throne room in her traditional white gown worn with a headdress of ostrich plumes, she saw Aly Khan. He took her breath away. Dark, handsome, resplendent in a white knee-length Indian tunic and a white turban fastened with a great emerald, he looked like a true Prince. She asked who he was and could not get him out of her mind. They met again soon after at a ball given by the Mountbattens at Brook House, danced together all that night and spent the rest of the summer demonstrating to everyone that they were very much in love. But Margaret Whigham's father said 'No' when they asked for his consent to marry. He thought they were far too young, and no doubt something of Aly's prowess as a lover had begun to filter through the social network. They met in secret for about six months, then Aly went out East and the affair came to an end.

Not long after the romance with Margaret Whigham, Aly became entangled with a woman ten years older than himself, the daughter of one of Britain's foremost peers. She was married to someone who bored and neglected her. Names were never mentioned but their love was said to be so intense and tempestuous that the Aga Khan, fearing a major scandal sent him to the United States to cool his ardour and get him out of the way. Ironically, the manoeuvre brought him into head-on collision with a royal rival.

At a dinner party in New York, Aly sat next to an elegant woman with the pale, hothouse beauty of a magnolia. Her name was Lady Thelma Furness. At that time she had been a 'close companion' of the Prince of Wales for four years. 'Aly immediately turned his battery of charm on me,' she recalled in her biography. By now Aly, aged 23, was a master tactician in the art of love. He persuaded her to dine with him the following evening. When he learned that she was due to sail back to England he begged her to delay her voyage so that he could accompany her. She laughingly protested that she must return according to plan.

On board ship she was staggered to find her cabin filled with red roses, each bouquet accompanied by a tender billet-doux: 'You left too soon, Aly', 'Love, Aly' and 'See you in London, Aly.' Next morning as she was having breakfast the telephone in her cabin rang. 'Hello, darling,' said a voice that sounded familiar. 'Will you have lunch with me today?' She was astonished to discover that he had sailed with her after all. She dined with him that evening and every evening until they docked at Southampton.

News that Thelma Furness was being ardently courted by Aly Khan reached England ahead of her. On her first evening back in London the Prince of Wales invited himself to her house. His manner was distinctly cool. 'I hear that Aly Khan has been very attentive to you,' he said in a clipped voice. It was the end of their relationship. Almost overnight she dropped out of his circle leaving Wallis Simpson to take her place.

Heartbroken at Edward's cool treatment of her, she flew to Aly for consolation. She joined him in Paris and they set off in his red sports car for a whirlwind tour of Europe. He was gay, attentive, impetuous and made love to her as only Aly knew how. The deeply wounded Thelma was made to feel as though she was the only woman in the world who mattered. He asked her to take over his villa at Deauville for the summer and bought her a horse at the Deauville sales. But as the days became cooler, so did his passion. He began seeing other women.

Rumour went round among the bluebloods that Aly Khan possessed some mysterious oriental love secret, for he was about to snaffle another daughter of the English aristocracy, this time Mrs Loel Guinness, wife of a wealthy young banker and daughter of Lord Churston. Joan Guinness had the thoroughbred look of the English debutante, tall, slim, haughty, but her great attraction was a dry sense of humour. In the summer of 1934 her husband was too occupied with business to be able to spend the entire holiday with his wife at Deauville. She was there alone when she met Aly at a dinner party. Her cool beauty intrigued him and her humour delighted him. He fell very deeply in love. Later that year he was cited as co-respondent in her divorce; three weeks after it was declared absolute, they were married in Paris.

Joan took the marriage very seriously. She wanted to share the whole of Aly's life so she became a Moslem and started to learn Eastern languages. She shared his love of horseracing. In every way she was an admirable wife. When their son, Karim, was born on 13 December 1936, their friends thought Aly had settled down for life. But he could never be a one-woman man.

He was fascinated by women of all social classes, backgrounds and nationalities whether they were single, divorced, married, prudish or worldly. He once said truthfully, 'I must have women around me . . . life means nothing to me without them.' But he sincerely believed that by marrying Joan Guinness, for whom he felt real love, that he would 'stay out of trouble' as he put it.

Instead, as the years went by it became downright fashionable to have an affair with Aly Khan and his prowess became the talk of the international set. It was said that a woman knew from the first moment whether or not he was interested. It was an electric, intensely physical communication, for at the bottom of Aly's success was sheer animal magnetism. He was, admitted many of his conquests, a marvellous lover in the physical sense. His remarkable staying powers were much envied. Apparently his father had sent him to a doctor in India as he approached manhood and he was taught the secret of how to control himself indefinitely and make love by the hour.

Wild stories circulated about the number of women he was supposed to make love to each day and for many years a story went the rounds of London that he plunged his arms up to the elbows in icy cold water in the course of an evening to rekindle his vitality. He was becoming a legend. Nothing, one felt, was impossible with Aly. Once interested he would grant a woman almost anything in the world she desired: diamonds, days basking in the Riviera sun or sailing in the Greek islands, parties in London or New York. He was magic.

His high life came to a temporary halt with the Second World War during which he performed a number of highly dangerous liaison missions and was commended for bravery in a citation signed by General de Gaulle. He was a British liaison officer with the American force that landed in the south of France in 1944. He at once drove along the coast road to Cannes and the Carlton Hotel. It had been closed for some time, but when Aly Khan turned up in uniform Jean Mero, the manager, threw open the doors, gave him the best suite on the first floor and declared the start of the post-war season!

When hostilities ceased he tried to pick up the threads of the life he had led before. To start with he bought a long, low white house near Nice called the Château de l'Horizon. It was in a terrible state and he started upon a massive renovation scheme during which he lived rough on the premises, roping in guests and staff to help. One night he received an invitation to a lavish party

THE WORLD'S GREATEST LOVERS

being given by Elsa Maxwell. For once he was not in the mood for company. He was tired and would have preferred a quiet supper alone. But Elsa Maxwell was not a lady to be put off easily. She told him she had invited a 'beautiful creature' especially for his benefit, a woman who would enchant him. Aly dressed and drove into town. He found himself being introduced to a stunningly beautiful redhead whose figure was sheathed in a skintight dress of shimmering white. He could not take his eyes off her. For once, it was Aly who was stunned. The girl was Rita Hayworth, the Hollywood star, married to Orson Welles.

After the party Aly took Rita on to a nightclub and in the next few weeks saw her nearly every day. She was so fascinated by him that she walked out on her career, risking a lawsuit from her studios so that she could go with him on his incessant wanderings. She soon learned that Aly could not bear life to stand still. It always had to be moving at the fastest possible pace. He had luxurious houses and flats on four continents, always ready for him to occupy.

There was a great deal of public scandal and criticism over the affair because Aly was still married to Joan and Rita to Orson Welles. The Aga Khan asked his son to bring Rita to meet him. The old man liked her shy manner and quiet voice, not at all what he had expected from a film star. He wrote later in his autobiography, 'I asked them if they were really devoted to each other. They said they were and I advised them to get married as soon as possible.'

Their divorces were hurried through and Aly planned a wedding the south of France was to remember for many years. The Château was lit from end to end with fairytale splendour; six hundred bottles of champagne were put on ice and gallons of eau de cologne poured into the swimming pool to perfume the night air. Hundreds of photographers scrambled after the glamorous couple on their honeymoon, hundreds of women sighed with envy as Aly gazed at his new wife with adoring eyes. The idyll seemed complete when Rita gave birth to their daughter, Yasmin, at a clinic in Lausanne on 2 December 1949.

But the marriage was already crumbling. Aly was appalled to discover that his beautiful wife longed to settle down to a quiet domestic life and bring up her daughter in one or other of his beautiful homes. He became bored with 'sitting around' and hankered for his old way of life. For a time Rita played along. She accompanied him on trips to Madrid, Casablanca, Marrakesh. Though she hated planes, she flew with him to Cairo in 1951 where they were entertained by King Farouk. She went on with him to Luxor, then Nairobi and Mombasa where Aly had religious ceremonies to supervise on behalf of his father. She could not take part in any of these affairs. As a non-Moslem female she could only stand by and wait. It was being brought home to her that she had married a man whose attitude to women, for all his European polish, was basically oriental. She was just an accessory, a very beautiful and admired accessory, but nothing more.

The final straw came when Aly, after finishing his duties with the Ismailis, went off on safari, leaving her behind. Furious, she went on a safari of her own. When they met again she had made up her mind to return to America with her daughter. Aly did not want to lose her and there were genuine attempts at reconciliation, but in January 1953, their marriage was dissolved in Reno.

Marital unheaval did not prevent him from escorting Joan Fontaine, the

Aly Khan and Rita Hayworth at their wedding

Bettina and Aly Khan

classically beautiful blonde actress, though she was said to have burst into tears over his contant attention to other women. He was also seen holding film star Gene Tierney in a close embrace as they danced and was said to have broken her heart. The Aga Khan was furious.

For once, Aly began to worry about his father's reaction. There had been disturbing rumours that the Aga might cut him out of the succession. Aly never really believed that he would do this. Ever since he was a child he had expected to follow in his father's footsteps. His life as a modern Don Juan seemed a separate thing to his life as a Moslem. He had travelled frequently as his father's representative, attending prayer services, dedicating schools and hospitals, greeting and counselling the people to whom the Aga was a god on earth.

But when the Aga Khan died in Geneva in the summer of 1957 Aly had the greatest shock of his life. When his father's will was read he learned that he had been passed over and his own son, Karim, had been chosen as the new Aga Khan.

Aly took this decision as a bitter blow. He was now in his mid-forties, still a very handsome man but inclined to paunchiness and thinning hair. Suddenly the life he was leading did not seem to add up to much. When he was asked to accept the post of United Nations delegate for Pakistan he agreed and in the short time left to him earned great respect for the work he did.

His attention was given more and more to one girl: Bettina, the Jacques Fath model whose beautiful figure, copper-coloured hair and freckled face had become the rage of Paris. They saw each other at various social gatherings, but for once Aly did not move in with his usual smooth routine. He waited, for this girl had a special quality.

Her real name was Simone Bodin. She was the daughter of a railwayman and had known something of poverty as a child. Brought up in Brittany as part of a large family, there was still something of the freshness of a country girl about her. Though she had left home to try to made a living as a dress designer in Paris, the great couturier Jacques Fath was attracted by her gamine looks, and persuaded her to change her name and become a model instead.

Aly began to escort her and gradually she became the most important part of his life. Though having a certain stillness about her she was always ready to fall in with his impetuous plans. He wanted to go to the races? Fine. She'd go with him. To the Riviera? Yes, she'd be ready in an hour. She took part in every aspect of his life and became, as the French so tactfully put it, 'the wife of his heart'. They could not marry for Rita Hayworth's Reno divorce was not recognized in France.

The end came with brutal suddenness. On the night of 12 May 1960 they were returning from a day's racing at Longchamps. Aly was at the wheel of his grey Lancia sports car. Coming in the opposite direction was a car with Belgian number plates. There was a scream of brakes as they met in head-on collision, then an awful silence. Bettina scrambled from the wreckage bleeding badly from a deep gash down the side of her face. But it was all over for the Eastern prince who had lost his birthright for the sake of love.

Porfirio Rubirosa

Señor Porfirio Rubirosa collected beautiful, wealthy women in the same way more prosaic men collect rare stamps. The suave Dominican diplomat was married five times, on two occasions to the richest women in the world, and he was once cited in a divorce court as the foreign co-respondent of the year.

In his prime he was a truly fascinating man with a lithe figure, brown complexion, dark hair slightly greying at the temples, high cheekbones, eyes slightly slanting and a dazzling smile. Combining his diplomatic skills with accomplished guitar playing, polo and dancing, he was the most sought after escort in fashionable resorts from Palm Beach to Cannes.

He flourished in the period immediately before and after the Second World War, which, as a social epoch, could well be remembered as the playboy years. It was the heyday of Aly Khan, the era of runaway heiresses and high society scandals. For all his amorous escapades and ferocious devotion to pleasure, Rubirosa was intelligent and likeable. His saving grace was a bubbling sense of humour. He could be in the middle of telling a story about himself and would suddenly collapse in fits of laughter because he had been taking himself too seriously.

Other men envied his stamina. He would keep a nightclub going into the early hours to amuse his guests then, fresher than anyone, he would be off for a ride on horseback as the sun rose. Like Aly Khan he drank Japanese mushroom tea for virility. Other men also eyed his lush apartments, private aeroplanes, strings of polo ponies, yachts and fast cars and rather meanly said he had married for money. But he was not a man's man. Smooth, suave, his nails as polished as his manners, he was the ladies' man par excellence.

Rubirosa was bored but polite when women threw themselves at him. He liked to make the running. Film stars attracted him and he escorted both Ava Gardner and Kim Novak; heiresses intrigued him and rich divorcées were offered a broad shoulder to weep on. But never, he claimed, had he felt guilt over a love affair. In spite of what people had said about him, he had never deliberately broken up a marriage. 'Many approaches have been made to me by married women. I have sent them away . . .' he wrote in his memoirs. 'Another thing – I have never talked about my affairs to other people. I do not boast of my conquests. I never reveal what you might call bedroom secrets.'

That supreme party hostess Elsa Maxwell said of him, 'You expect Rubi to be a very dangerous young man who personifies the wolf. Instead, you meet someone who is so unbelievably charming and thoughtful that you are put offguard before you know it.'

Porfirio Rubirosa was one of four children born to a Dominican family that knew nothing of the kind of glamorous life to which he was to grow accustomed. He joined the Army when he was old enough and rose to the rank of captain by the time he was 20. He might have remained an obscure officer in Central America, but one day when he trotted out with his Army team to play a game of polo, Flor de Oro Trujillo, the plump, 16-year-old daughter of Dominican dictator Rafael Trujillo, was watching from the stands. Flor de Oro (Flower of Gold) liked what she saw. She asked to meet him.

After a clandestine romance during which Trujillo, trying to keep the young pair apart, first transferred Rubirosa to a remote fortress, then dismissed him from the Army, they were married. 'Rubi', as he was generally known, had won the respect of his father-in-law and that was no mean feat. Until his murder in 1961 Generalissimo Trujillo was the most feared dictator in Central America.

Rubi had made his first good match and was on his way to fame and fortune. He had 50,000 dollars in the bank, a brand new Packard and a job in the Dominican foreign office. To start him off on his diplomatic career, Trujillo decided to send him to Berlin. Flor went too, but she soon tired of sitting in the background while exquisitely dressed, sophisticated women in the diplomatic set crowded round the newcomer. Little 'Flower of Gold' packed her bags and went back to the Dominican Republic to find herself a husband with less charisma. Their marriage had lasted only five years. Rubirosa said many years later, 'I think Flor would agree that we knew nothing then about life or love. We were too young . . .'

Trujillo, far from venting his paternal wrath, sent Rubi to Paris as Chargé d'Affaires. He was then 32 and had already acquired a reputation as a lover. Women began to accept invitations to parties just because they knew he would be there.

Just before the war he went to a cocktail party on the Left Bank. Through the haze of cigarette smoke his eyes sought out the most beautiful woman in the room. It was Danielle Darrieux, darling of the French cinema. They did not meet but at the end of the party he was asked if he could give her a lift home.

'Be careful, Danielle,' another friend called cheerfully. 'That man is dangerous.'

'Is he really!' she called back with that famous tinkling laugh.

They fell madly, romantically in love, were married in 1942 and lived through the German occupation together. During the war Rubi clashed several times with the German authorities and was sent to a prison camp at Bad Nauheim for punching a German officer in a nightclub. He weathered the imprisonment well but in 1944 was involved in a mysterious affair in which he was shot and wounded by an unknown gunman in a Paris street. He was taken to hospital with three bullets in him and for a time hovered between life and death while the beautiful, dark-haired Danielle kept watch by his bedside.

Once he was out of danger she suggested they went to the Riviera where he could recuperate. It was a mistake. The war was over in Europe and the international set had flooded back to the old haunts in all its glory. Rubi recovered and was soon back on form. Women flocked round him. One Argentine beauty chased him until her jealous husband challenged Rubirosa to a duel, an offer he swiftly declined. Danielle found herself kicking her heels in their sumptuous hotel suite, waiting for him to come home.

Back in Paris she returned to her acting career and they just drifted apart.

'There was no scene,' he told someone later. 'We just talked quietly and sadly and said goodbye.'

Their divorce came through in 1947 but by then Rubi was already courting the woman who was to be his third wife. This time he hit the jackpot. The love of his heart was Doris Duke, heiress to a tobacco fortune estimated at 300 million dollars. She was one of the richest, if not the richest, woman in the world at that time. Tall and blonde, he liked her because she was such good fun and full of life, unlike so many of the wealthy beauties who hung around him. He married her soon after his divorce from Danielle and for a wedding present she gave him a twin-engined aircraft fitted out with five big armchairs, a bed and a fully-trained pilot. She joined him in the kind of life he relished, including endless parties. He really came into his own at parties. Starting off quietly, he slowly built up a head of steam. After several of the lethal rum cocktails which he had specially mixed for him, he would often perform an Apache dance on his own, sing snatches of songs and launch into a routine that caused great hilarity. Once he finished his act by jumping into a swimming pool fully-clothed and doing the crawl to the other side while still singing at the top of his voice. It was reported that when he got out, dripping wet, he still looked well groomed.

The marriage with Doris Duke lasted barely two years and broke up, he said, because she drove him insane with her insatiable appetite for jazz. Day and night, he complained, she hammered away at the piano. Rubirosa fled.

Their relationship could not have been improved by rumours drifting around the diplomatic world about Rubi and Eva Peron. For a short time Rubirosa's duties took him to the Argentine. When he went to present his credentials to Eva Peron, wife of the all-powerful dictator Juan Peron, she surveyed him coolly. 'I believe you divorce rather frequently, Your Excellency,' she said. He needed all his diplomacy to answer that one. According to his memoirs, he took a deep breath and answered, 'When things no longer go according to plan, when quarrels are frequent, when life together is a trial rather than a pleasure, it is better to separate.' She eyed him with interest. After that first meeting he began to see the extraordinary, beautiful Eva often. Too often. Trujillo did not like the reports that were coming back to him. Rubirosa's meetings with Eva had been noted and talked about among other diplomats. He was treading on dangerous ground and Trujillo recalled him.

Scarcely taking time to draw breath, he was soon immersed in his next affair, this time with the vivacious Hungarian-born film star Zsa Zsa Gabor. Her husband, George Sanders, was said to be furious. They appeared all over Paris together and she admitted going to his house, tucked away in a discreet corner of the city, for intimate dinners for two. There were newspaper stories about their forthcoming engagement and she prattled merrily about a diamond ring. But though he was obviously fascinated by this blonde bombshell, he found her much too strong-willed for his liking and there was no marriage.

In May 1953 Rubi was sacked from his post as Chargé d'Affaires because he had been named as co-respondent in the divorce case of Robert Sweeney, the golfer. But he was soon given it back again when he suddenly announced that he was about to marry Woolworth heiress Barbara Hutton.

From the very beginning no one believed this marriage would work out. Rubirosa had never looked better, his dark hair greying at the temples, his figure lithe as a matador's through regular exercise in his own gym, his rakish charm still as effective as ever. Barbara Hutton, on the other hand had become known as America's 'poor little rich girl', a sad, pale-faced heiress dripping in diamonds and sables who seemed to be forever searching for love.

She became Rubirosa's fourth wife but their marriage lasted a mere 72 days. On their honeymoon, while his bride was nursing a broken ankle, Rubi escorted

Rubirosa marries Doris Duke, 'the richest girl in the world'

beautiful girls round the nightclubs. 'It's a kind of reflex action,' he shrugged. It was a marriage that was over before it began. 'There was nothing I could do to beat off the sickness and sadness that engulfed her,' he said when it was over. She was a delightful and charming person, but she would not face the sunshine. She liked to stay in her room even though the doctors urged her to get out into the fresh air. 'I couldn't live like that. She was not rich, she was poor. My God, there are so many women richer . . .'

She gave him a plane, a farm and a string of polo ponies when they married and £300,000 at the divorce. He swore that he would never again marry a wealthy woman. Wealthy women were too difficult. Many felt that he should never have proposed to Barbara Hutton in the first place and the accusation that he did it for money stuck hard.

He was 46 when 18-year-old French actress Odile Rodin came into his life. He met her when she was comparatively unknown, acting in a play by Marcel Pagnol at a Paris theatre. She was an entrancing girl with deep blue eyes, pale gold hair and a body as slim as a reed. She had no fortune. When her friends saw that Rubirosa was deeply interested in her they feared she was in for a lot of heartache.

They married in 1956 when she was 19 and cynical observers gave them six months. But they did not know Odile Rodin. She had nothing but herself to bring to the marriage, but after nine years there was no hint of a break up, no gossip, no scandal. She had persuaded the great playboy to settle down.

His house in Paris was sold and they bought an 18th-century villa standing in its own park in the village of Marnes la Coquette, just seven miles from the city. He had always protested that he liked home life but nobody had believed him. 'I like setting up a home. I like arranging a garden and helping my wife to choose furniture,' he protested. With Odile he arranged Louis XVI furniture, hung original paintings by Fragonard and Watteau, and chose lime silk hangings and chair covers to go with deep white carpets. They seemed very happy.

'I knew I was marrying a Don Juan,' said Odile, 'but to know is to be forewarned and I am determined to be the last of his wives.' Her words were sadly prophetic.

On 5 July 1965 at an hour when most Parisians were brewing coffee for breakfast he was on his way home from an all night polo party. No one knows exactly what happened, but his 150 mph grey Ferrari sports car crashed into a tree after rebounding from a parked car. It was not far from the spot where Aly Khan met his end in a similar fashion. Rubi was trapped in the wreckage, his chest crushed by the steering wheel. He was dead on arrival at hospital.

Odile Rubirosa had left the party three hours earlier and had tried to persuade him to go with her. When she was told what had happened she could only whisper. 'It was fate.'

Rubirosa and
Zsa Zsa Gabor

Rubirosa with Odile Rodin at
their villa outside Paris

Francisco Pignatari

When Francisco Pignatari walked into any top nightclub or restaurant in Paris, London, Rome or New York, everything stopped for a split second. Men stared, women whispered and waiters hovered as the tall, bronzed Brazilian escorted his latest beautiful companion to the best table. There would be red roses for her. Always red roses from 'Baby' Pignatari. He had sent armfuls to ex- Queen Soraya of Persia when he was trying to woo her, to Princess Monica of Liechtenstein, to Princess Ira, to stars like Linda Christian and Rosanna Schiaffino. There would be champagne, of course. Perhaps a gift of diamonds. Then the ride home, when Baby might well decide to drive his Mercedes from the back seat using his toes, or zoom round moonlit bends at 95 mph.

Women who allowed themselves to be captured by this daredevil gallant, this fantastically wealthy man who earned his money by working for it, had to learn to live dangerously. For Pignatari, hero of the international champagne set in the fifties and sixties, was no boudoir Romeo, no ordinary playboy.

To start with, he could woo in French, Spanish, Italian, German, English and Portuguese. High-powered and hard-working, he built up Brazil's third biggest industrial empire, then, when he felt that he had done enough, he played as hard as he had worked. But Baby had a wild streak. He loved to go fast in cars, planes, speedboats and motorbikes. He smashed up 25 cars then stopped counting.

Three times he tried marriage and tried hard to settle down with one woman, but those who knew him said it was like trying to bottle dynamite.

Pignatari was given the nickname 'Baby' as a child and, whether he liked it or not, it stuck. Brought up in São Paulo, he became the favourite of Brazilian society when he was very young. His mother was the daughter of Count Francisco Matarazzo, head of Brazil's greatest industrial family; his father was an oculist, Dr Julio Pignatari, who abandoned his profession when he married and tried to be a tycoon, too. Baby thought of nothing but pleasure until the day he learned his father was dying. Then, realizing how much it had cost him to try to keep up with the Matarazzos, he promised he would take over his mill with its 400 employees and run it himself.

So, to the astonishment of high society, in 1937 when he was 20 years old, Baby Pignatari went to work. His titled mother was horrified at the thought of her handsome, spoiled son getting involved with manual labour. But he left the house at six o'clock every morning, however late he had been to bed the night before, and workmen stared in amazement as he set to and swept floors and oiled machinery. They came to admire him as he turned into a brilliant engineer and built up an industrial empire making everything from machine guns to pots and pans and employing thousands.

'I don't mind being called a millionaire playboy,' he said once. 'But I like people to know that I worked hard for my money. I worked ten or twelve hours a day for 23 years. Then I decided it was time I had a little fun.'

The fun began in earnest and his hobby became the pursuit of beautiful women. He kept a book with a note of his conquests and those he wanted to contact again. It contained the names of some of the most famous beauties in Europe and America. Eventually he hired an Englishman, Richard Gully, as his secretary, to keep track of his dates and send red roses, twenty dozen at a time, to his latest love.

Pignatari married twice before becoming the world's No 1 playboy. His first wife was Italian society beauty Mimosa Delfino, by whom he had a son. His second was lovely Brazilian heiress Nelita de Lima, with whom he was deeply in love. But both marriages ended in divorce after seven years, though he had the highest regard for both his wives. He declared he would never marry again. 'It is like being in prison, like being locked up in a cell,' he groaned.

By 1959 he was undisputed champion in the playboy stakes. He would sit down for lunch in some famous international restaurant and before he got to the coffee he would have collected half a dozen beautiful women, some titled, all drawn by his charm. He had a superb villa in the exclusive Italian resort of Forte dei Marmi where his guests could arrive by plane, train, or in his chauffeur-driven Rolls Royce. He kept a Mercedes sports car in Hollywood so that he could pick up any beauty he had his eye on at a moment's notice.

Stories were circulating about his high-speed wooing. The moment beautiful Queen Soraya was a free woman, after the Shah's decision to take a new wife, Baby rushed in with red roses, dozens of them sent to her from wherever he happened to be. Friends said he had always admired her. They had met first in Switzerland, then in Rome and he invited her to his superb mansion in Rio. There were rumours that he had proposed, but the friendship went no further.

He once hired the whole of the exclusive Calypso Beach outside Rome for the day, just so that he could have actress Jackie Lane to himself without the other sunbathers around, and he wooed Tyrone Power's ex wife, actress Linda Christian, across four continents.

The affair with Linda Christian was stormy and headline-catching, and it was probably the fact that they both enjoyed a good fight that kept them attracted to each other. One night, after a party, Pignatari went to collect his car and was just in time to catch Linda letting down his tyres. They had quarrelled over some trivial matter. In the tussle that followed, Linda lost one of the beautiful gold

'Baby' Pignatari with his second wife, the former Princess Ira von Furstenberg

and green jade earrings she was wearing. In a second, Baby was all concern. Where had she bought them? Hong Kong? They would go there right away and try to find a match, or a pair similar. Before she could protest, they were on their way, taking in Rome, Athens, Cairo and Bangkok before their shopping spree in Hong Kong. When they finally got back to his home town, São Paulo, a euphoric Linda began telling everyone how much in love they were, how she hoped they would soon be engaged. Baby was irked by this sort of possessive behaviour. He had no intention of being tied down again. He suddenly had a brilliant idea and hired pickets to walk round and round her hotel with placards reading 'Linda Go Home'. She was furious, but he refused to admit he had behaved in a manner not befitting a Brazilian gentleman and laughed uproariously at the traffic jam he had caused. It was not the end of their romance, however. When he met her in New York he was full of apologies for his prank and tried to organize a 'Linda Please Stay' parade – but he couldn't find any pickets.

Baby was always generous to women, and to himself. One Christmas he gave himself a ten-piece set of alligator skin luggage, a Bentley Continental, a Rolls Royce, a Mercedes, 30 Savile Row suits, 60 silk shirts, 6 skiing outfits, 3 cowboy outfits and some ten gallon hats to be worn on his Brazilian ranch.

Powerfully built, 6ft 3ins tall and full of vitality, he had to let off steam every now and them. He courted and loved danger, sometimes behaving like a madman. His favourite party piece, when he had a pretty girl in the passenger seat, was suddenly to lever himself into the back of the car and drive with his feet. Sometimes he would take girls up in his private plane and dive down to clip the tops off tall, leafy trees with the propellor. He would ride a motorbike at 50 mph standing on the saddle with his arms folded. The only time he came near to death was when he took his motorlaunch up to top speed and turned it over in the Pacific rollers. The boat was smashed to driftwood and Pignatari, having gone through the windscreen, had to be rushed to hospital.

At the height of his popularity as a playboy in 1960 Baby Pignatari fell madly in love again, this time with the luscious little Princess Ira von Fürstenberg. Princess Ira, whose family owns the Italian Fiat works, made world headlines when, at the age of 15 she married German-born Prince Alfonso of Hohenlohe in a memorable, fairytale wedding. But the magic had worn off. When Baby started to woo her, the 20-year-old Princess had no defence. She fell in love with him after a wild courtship and they ran away together. Baby chartered a yacht from King Farouk of Egypt and took Princess Ira and 30 guests for a cruise in the Red Sea. The Princess had been warned by her husband that if she continued to see Pignatari she would never see her children again.

She was too much in love to take the threat seriously and they eloped to Mexico City. After some very ugly scenes when Prince Alfonso tried to hold on to his two sons, Princess Ira got her divorce and married her Brazilian lover.

The marriage lasted three years. They were still in love with each other when Baby set off for Reno to arrange their separation. The trouble was that the young mother could not forget her children and the only way she could gain custody of them was by leaving Pignatari. He understood and the whole thing was arranged without bitterness.

This really marked the end of him as an international playboy. Still, one likes to think of him showing privileged friends into his huge bedroom where on an illuminated glass shelf stood a solitary white, high heeled shoe. 'A trophy,' he would chuckle, 'of one that nearly got away.'

Chapter
Seven

LITERARY LOVERS

George Bernard Shaw

George Bernard Shaw, one of the greatest philanderers in the world of literature, came to the conclusion that the best love affairs were those conducted by post. His romance with Ellen Terry, the most acclaimed actress of her generation and the darling of English theatre with her sweet face, charm and vitality, lasted for 26 years. Yet it was only after thousands of words had passed between them that she saw him for the first time through a peephole in the Lyceum curtain. Shaw, sitting in his usual drama critic's seat in the stalls, was completely unaware of the fact that he was being scrutinized. She wrote to him that night, 'What a boy you are! What a duck!'

The letters started in the 1890s when Ellen Terry wrote to him in his capacity as music critic of the *World* magazine and asked him to give his opinion on a young singer she knew. Shaw answered in detail and their correspondence went on from there almost until Ellen Terry's death.

Week by week their affection for each other deepened. Shaw had been enchanted by the actress from the moment he saw her. Now he became very resentful towards the great actor-manager, Henry Irving, who had her under contract and, in Shaw's opinion, was wasting her wonderful talent. She sought to bring them together but with little success.

For a time the pen and paper lovers were content not to meet. But inevitably the theatre brought them together. When they came face to face it was usually in public and both were usually nervous on these occasions. Shaw, writing after one such encounter to his 'blessedest, darling Ellen', said it was because people were watching them and 'the way I want to, and ought to behave, would be ridiculous and indecorous'. He promised not to spoil his high regard for her by 'philandering follies', but warned her she had better 'keep out of my reach'. The Shaw–Terry letters now rank among the classic correspondences of all time.

Until the age of 29, Bernard Shaw remained celibate, though he had been quite normally susceptible to pretty women from adolescence. He attributed his chastity to two factors: poverty and fastidiousness.

He wrote an extraordinary letter to his friend Frank Harris on the subject in 1930: 'If you have any doubts as to my virility, dismiss them from your mind. I was not impotent, I was not sterile. I was not homosexual and I was extremely, though not promiscuously, susceptible.' And he assured him, 'I never associated sexual intercourse with delinquency. I associated it always with delight.' After the age of 29, he said, he tried all the experiments and learned what there was to be learned from them. 'After that date,' he added, 'I did not pursue women. I was pursued by them.'

As a young man Shaw was not particularly attractive. Over six feet tall, painfully thin, with slatey blue eyes in a pale face, rusty red hair parted in the middle and a rather straggly red beard, he looked awkward and undernourished. He improved enormously as the years went by. He filled out, sported a splendid beard and generally grew better looking. Once he started to talk, he was arresting. Contemporaries said it was impossible to convey a true impression of his vivid charm and the spell cast by his voice with its soft, Irish lilt.

At his most active philandering stage he had more than his share of vitality. The early days of his association with the Fabian Society saw him with seven women in tow. He had his work cut out to stop them bumping into each other. And all the time he was flirting with someone or other by post.

Bernard Shaw was born in Synge Street, Dublin, on 26 July 1856. His mother was a hard working, impassive gentlewoman who had to shoulder all the responsibility shrugged off by her drunken but amiable father. Music was her consolation, and in 1872, leaving her 15-year-old son to live with his father in lodgings, she packed her bags and set off for London where she thought her talents as a singing teacher would be better appreciated. Her two daughters went with her, though one died soon after. Later in life he told Ellen Terry, 'Oh, a devil of a childhood, Ellen, rich only in dreams, frightful and loveless in realities.'

Shaw worked for an estate agent when he left school, but at the age of 20, having come to the conclusion there was no future for him in Dublin, he joined his mother in England. At first he lived on sufferance with her and his priggish sister, Lucy, at Victoria Grove, Chelsea. He considered banking and the civil service as a career but neither appealed to him. He wanted above all things to be a novelist and in the next five years wrote five books, none successful. The little money he did earn came from occasional jobs as a freelance journalist.

While writing a novel called *Cashel Byron's Profession* he fell in love for the first time. The object of his desire was one of his mother's pupils, a Sunday school teacher called Alice Lockett. Their romance began rather tepidly in March 1882 and, according to Shaw, 'gathered momentum' over a period of two years. She must have been a girl of some character to have held Shaw for that long, but theirs was a milk-and-water affair compared with what followed.

Alice passed out of his life to marry a doctor. The next woman to attract him was a very different proposition. Mrs Jenny Patterson, another of his mother's pupils, was 15 years older than him, a good looking, well-to-do widow with submerged passions. He would escort her home to her house in Brompton Square, staying later and later each night until on his 29th birthday at three o'clock in the morning, according to his diary, he was 'seduced and raped'. He admitted, 'I found I liked sexual intercourse because of its amazing power of producing a celestial flood of emotion and exaltation of existence.' But he was soon to know the other side of Jenny Patterson. She had an extremely jealous and possessive temperament. For eight years she clung to him, creating scenes, invading his home, throwing fits of hysteria and resenting any other woman. He always meant to break with her but could never bring himself to do it.

Shaw became an enthusiastic socialist, an active member of the Fabian Society in its hey-day, and that organization was full of attractive young women who found the newly confident, silver-tongued Irishman quite fascinating. At one socialist soirée he met Florence Farr, a young actress full of progressive ideas. She was also pretty and sympathetic – his ideal of the truly feminine – and he fell head over heels in love with her. Florence was one of the 'new women', living apart from her husband, refusing help from her parents and earning her living as a career woman on the stage. When Shaw had finished his first play, *Widowers' Houses*, he asked Florence to be leading lady. And though he discovered she had had many lovers before him he was still enchanted enough to write, 'You are my best and dearest love, the regenerator of my heart, the holiest joy of my soul, my treasure, my salvation, my rest, my reward, my darling youngest child, my secret glimpse of heaven.' Shaw was never short of words even when it came to love.

One night when they were together, Jenny Patterson burst in upon them, hysterically attacking the young actress. Shaw tried to remonstrate with her, but it took two hours to get her out of the house. The ugly scene at last convinced him that his affair with Jenny must come to an end. She continued to shower him with letters for months but he returned them all, unopened and unread.

He saw Florence as his ideal leading lady. She was a good actress, but he tried to turn her into a great one by bullying and preaching. He gave her the plum part of 'Louka' in *Arms and the Man*, which was a huge success, but it was the last play of his in which she appeared. His ardour was cooling. Eventually the poet W.B. Yeats snatched her away. 'Yeats was such a handsome man I knew I hadn't an earthly,' said Shaw, yet one suspects that he was ready to try his charms in fresh pastures.

No sooner had Florence vanished from his life than he was making love to another actress, Janet Achurch, who was married to Charles Charrington, an admired actor. Infatuation must have affected his critical eye for he wrote *Candida* for her, calling her 'the greatest actress on earth'. Janet apparently had a weakness for gin and more than once he had to calm her down before a performance. She and her husband had flaming rows about Shaw and after one of them Charrington yelled, 'You can have Janet. You've destroyed everything.'

Unrepentant at having played cuckoo-in-the-nest in the Charrington

George Bernard Shaw

Ellen Terry

household, he now contemplated the conquest of one of the most famous women in England – Annie Besant. She was a very serious-minded creature, full of causes and unorthodox opinions, but very graceful and compelling. She had been married to a clergyman at 20 but found being a vicar's wife too restricting for her active brain. There was so much she disagreed with. When she told her horrified husband she could no longer take the sacrement he told her to leave. She hated Victorian convention and preached birth control, atheism and women's rights. Pamphlets poured from her pen. Shaw converted her to socialism and was not a bit frightened of her. They grew very close.

Annie felt they were drifting towards an affair, and in order to regularize the growing intimacy between them, drew up a deed which was like some sort of marriage contract. She was still married to the Rev Frank Besant but brushed that fact aside. When Shaw read Annie's marriage document he burst out laughing. 'Good God, this is worse than all the vows exacted by all the churches on earth!' Unfortunately, Annie did not have a sense of humour and was deeply hurt by his reaction. She would not alter a word of it, so it was agreed they would have to go their separate ways. She took the parting badly and swore he had turned her hair prematurely grey.

Leading socialist Beatrice Webb was one of the few Fabian women who did not hanker after Shaw at some time or other. 'You cannot be in love with a sprite and Shaw is a sprite in such matters, not a real person,' she observed shrewdly.

As if to prove what she said, Shaw next got himself involved in a 'mystical marriage' with the daughter of William Morris, the great craftsman-designer. Shaw had spent a Sunday evening dining at the Morris's beautiful house in Hammersmith which was decorated with furniture and fabrics of medieval inspiration. He was about to leave when May Morris walked into the hall. He felt as though he had been struck by lightning. She was tall, dark, striking, dressed in pre-Raphaelite style. 'I looked at her, rejoicing in her lovely dress and lovely self; and she looked at me and made a gesture of assent with her eyes. I was immediately conscious that a mystical betrothal was registered in heaven . . .'

The whole thing remained on a mystical plane for so long, however, that May Morris, tired of waiting for Shaw to do something, married writer Henry Halliday Sparling. Shaw would not leave the couple alone and when there was eventually a divorce, he narrowly missed being named as co-respondent. The trouble was, May Morris wore her heart on her sleeve and everyone knew she was mad about Shaw. When he failed to scoop her up on the second opportunity, the whole thing ended rather bitterly.

Observing these amorous exploits, Sidney Webb, great socialist and husband of Beatrice, exclaimed, 'My! Shaw, you do warm both hands at the fire of life.'

Shaw was one of the few people in England who had actually read Karl Marx, so he was intrigued when he began to encounter Eleanor Marx, his younger daughter, in the reading room of the British Museum. 'Tussy', as her father called her, had flyaway black hair, fine black eyes and a musical voice. She was an affectionate, clever, sensitive girl and they became great friends. For two years Shaw continued to see Eleanor Marx and dither about their relationship. She was snatched from under his nose by Dr Edward Aveling, a leading atheist and Marxist, who was already married. The whole thing ended tragically. Eleanor killed herself. Shaw never forgave Dr Aveling.

One woman who openly pursued him was Edith Nesbit, who was married to the highly promiscuous Hubert Bland (he installed his mistresses and illegitimate children under their family roof). She fell head over heels in love with Shaw and his 'maddening white face'. E. Nesbit, as she was always known, the author of delightful children's books still popular today, was a tall, restless, good-humoured woman, but she did not arouse a corresponding passion in Shaw. He took her for long walks, gave her tea at the British Museum and discussed politics with her. But when she turned up alone at his place in Fitzroy Square he behaved with ungentlemanly alarm and asked her to leave. He decided the only way to cure Edith was to bore her to death, so he treated her to lengthy monologues on economics. They remained very good friends.

Marriage was something that Shaw had never really considered essential for his well being, but in the summer of 1896, while staying with the Webbs at Saxmundham, he had met a 34-year-old Irish heiress who, despite her millions, had joined the Fabian Society. 'I am going to refresh my heart by falling in love with her,' he wrote to Ellen Terry. Charlotte Payne-Townshend was a large, graceful woman with masses of brown hair, green eyes and a pleasant expression. She was well on the way to becoming an old maid.

Charlotte and Shaw came to like each other very much. She often surprised him. For instance, though a quiet and private sort of person, she had been a friend of Lawrence of Arabia. Early in 1898 she became Shaw's private secretary. From his letters it was clear that marriage was on his mind but Charlotte's wealth bothered him. He felt he could not go into a partnership unless he had prospects of financial success, enough to make him independent of her money.

His millionairess set off on a world tour with the Webbs, leaving him to contemplate the future. The tourists had only reached Rome when a telegram arrived saying Shaw was seriously ill. Without delay, Charlotte turned round and came back. She found him in appalling conditions, languishing in a room cluttered with books, thick with dust and smelling of the congealed remains of meals that had not been taken away. He was ill from overwork and an abcess which had caused a necrosis of the bone in one of his feet.

Charlotte acted at once. She whisked him away to a house she had rented in Surrey where he was properly fed and tended by a doctor. After a time he became worried that he might be compromising her. He tentatively suggested they should be married. Charlotte acted again. She went straight out and bought the ring and a licence.

On 1 June 1898 they were married, Shaw hobbling to his nuptials on crutches. Charlotte settled down to the business of looking after her genius. The marriage was very curious. Charlotte was not interested in sex at all but Shaw said if necessary he could find that sort of experience elsewhere. Their relationship was comfortable, platonic, wholesome. Though she resolutely refused to consummate the marriage, Charlotte managed the house smoothly and efficiently providing comfort, order and regular vegetarian meals. Shaw treated Charlotte with patience and consideration, but he did not stop philandering.

There can be no doubt that he was often pursued quite relentlessly. The saga of Erica Cotterill shows the almost comic aspect of some of his dallying. She lived on a farm in Devon but read avidly and conceived a great admiration for Shaw as a writer. She became gripped with a frenzied desire to meet him. When she wrote him an unusually intelligent fan letter he could not resist answering at length. Her requests for a meeting grew more and more persistent until, at last, Shaw reluctantly agreed.

She arrived at the peaceful hamlet of Ayot St Lawrence, where Shaw lived, riding a motorbike. He was horrified and begged her to go away. Instead she found lodgings at a cottage in the village and got a message through to Shaw saying that she would even sleep in the fields if it meant she could be near him. Thoroughly alarmed by this intense young woman, he went to his wife for assistance. The next time Erica called at the house Charlotte was waiting for her. She turned her away, forbidding her to come near the house again. She did turn up sometimes, quite unexpectedly and Shaw lived in a state of uncertainty listening for her motorbike. Years later her wrote, 'Erica Cotterill imagined herself violently in love with me and, being about one-third quite mad, was a terror and a nuisance. She would arrive on a motorcycle and assume my house was her own and I her husband . . . but she was an exquisite sort of person and had literary talent!'

Shaw's marriage was never really threatened, except by one woman, the famous actress, Mrs Patrick Campbell. Charlotte often complained that Shaw was 'always writing to Ellen' but she didn't really mind. Mrs Campbell worried and upset her.

Stella Beatrice Campbell had taken London by storm in *The Second Mrs Tanqueray*. She was temperamental, shrewish and selfish but when she put her mind to it she could also seem like the most fascinating woman on earth, quite capable of answering Shaw's wit with sallies of her own. He wrote *Pygmalion* for her, knowing that as Eliza Higgins she would be a sensation, especially in the scenes which were meant to shock. When Sir Herbert Tree, who was playing Professor Higgins, suggested at lunch one day giving Shaw a beefsteak 'to put some red blood in him' Stella retorted, 'For God's sake, no. If you give him meat no woman in London will be safe.'

Shaw wooed his Stella by letter at first, but it was not enough. He went out of his way to seek her company and to his horror, at the age of 56 fell madly and hopelessly in love with her. His letters to her were passionate and committed. There were phone calls which betrayed his feelings. Charlotte heard one of them by accident and sensed danger. Shaw threw his hands to heaven and asked, 'Why cannot one make one beloved woman happy without sacrificing another?' When Stella complained that as a critic he had maligned her for years he wrote back, 'Dearest Liar – never did a man paint his infatuation across the heavens more rapturously and shamelessly.'

There was a moment when he could have swept her off her feet, but he hesitated, as he always did in emotional matters, and the next thing he knew she was in the arms of George Cornwallis West, the handsome Edwardian playboy. He never forgave her. He had risked everything, risked Charlotte's happiness and peace of mind. 'I', he thundered, 'I, the greatest living master of letters made a perfect spectacle of myself with her before all Europe.'

After Stella his philandering was never the same. They still wrote to each other, but her career began to slide and tragedy came into her life. As an old woman of 75, living in France, her last letter to him began, 'Dear, dear Joey'.

Shaw, of course, went on to greater fame and lived to be revered, though he used his great age – he was still working at his typewriter when he was 90 – as an excuse for saying the most outrageous things. 'I have always believed myself to be exceptionally attractive to women,' he would say, stroking his white beard. 'Whenever I have been left alone in a room with a susceptible female, she has invariably thrown her arms around me and declared she adored me.'

Charlotte died in 1943 after they had been together for 45 years. In his last days Shaw had a splendid Scottish housekeeper to fend off marauding females. He fell when pruning an apple tree in the garden of Ayot St Lawrence, broke his leg and died on 2 November 1950 from the complications that followed.

Frank Harris

My Life and Loves by Frank Harris caused an uproar. Nobody had ever written an autobiography quite as violently physical before. Of course he told outrageous lies, absolute whoppers, about his sex life. But it was all there in black and white, in hair-raising detail, and in the best circles it was decided that Frank Harris was a bounder and a cad.

In fact Harris was brilliant, probably the most dynamic writer of his day, a shrewd observer of the world and only according to himself the most prolific sexual athlete since Casanova.

When the first volume of *My Life and Loves* was published in 1925 it was regarded as pornography and suppressed. The second volume shocked because it exposed the habits and behaviour of some very important people. Harris was shunned by decent women, ignored in his club, and thoroughly appreciated by George Bernard Shaw. Harris, said Shaw, was born an outlaw and would never be anything else, but he had 'a high regard for the ruffian'.

To look at he was almost ugly. He was short and thick set, with a bold jaw and aggressive nose. His black hair grew thick and low on his forehead and he had fine, dark moustaches. His expression was often surly. His height caused him concern and he used 'lifts' in his shoes to try to make himself seem taller. His great physical attraction was his voice, which was deep, resonant and used with force and vigour when neccessary.

Hesketh Pearson, that marvellous chronicler of extraordinary people, said that topographically and temperamentally Frank Harris was born all over the place. His date of birth, varied from 14 February 1854 to 14 February 1856. He stuck to St Valentine's Day throughout because the association pleased him, but he possibly, said Pearson, who knew him, made that up as well. He was probably born in Tenby, North Wales, but sometimes, for a change, he insisted it was Galway in Ireland or Brighton in Sussex.

His bullying father was a captain in the Navy and as a child Frank hated him. He had two brothers and a sister and they were all looked after by a nurse. One day Frank caught the nurse in bed with a man and when she next refused to let him have sugar on his bread and butter he threatened to tell.

Frank's appreciation of female anatomy began at school where he would constantly drop pencils, pens and india rubbers so that he could crawl under the desks and examine the girls' legs.

He ran away to America when he was fourteen and worked as a labourer on the construction of Brooklyn Bridge, as a hotel porter in Chicago and a cowpuncher in Texas. Having earned some money, he decided to further his education and spent a year at Kansas University, dividing his time between the classics and seducing the prettier girl students. He was later called to the Bar.

Eventually he arrived back in England, visited his family and found that he liked his father after all. He spent a year as a master at Brighton College, made some money by gambling in shares, then travelled in Germany and Greece.

Harris seldom failed to get what he wanted when he concentrated all his efforts. He longed to conquer the literary world and he longed to conquer women. He gave much study to the craft of arousing desire and seemed to have no difficulty in carrying his studies through to their natural conclusion.

He returned to London in the early 1880s and 'by the cunning pursuit of men and the amorous pursuit of women' he obtained the editorship of the *Evening News* in 1882. He says in his autobiography that he began by assuming that his readers would be as mentally adult as himself. Finding they were not, he lowered the level. Again he failed, so he decided the average newspaper reader had the tastes and intelligence of a boy of fourteen and concentrated on the things that had attracted him at that age – sex, crime and sport. By the end of one week he had nearly doubled the circulation. He went on to become editor of the *Fortnightly Review*, a highly respected and dignified paper. People in the literary world were then forced to take him seriously, though they never could find out how he got the job in the first place. They suspected a feminine influence.

Though he had hundreds of passing affairs, Harris came closest to being in love when he met a girl called Laura Clapton. Very little is known about her, but obviously she did not respond to Frank's usual Casanova routine. He was extremely jealous when he saw her with another man. They never married but he could not get her out of his system and their affair went on for years.

During one of his separations from Laura he became very friendly with Mrs Edith Clayton, a wealthy widow who loved to entertain famous and eminent people in her Park Lane house. Harris had been asked to stand as Tory MP for Hackney and came to the conclusion that the easiest way to finance his efforts was by marrying Mrs Clayton. He wooed and won her but, as everyone expected, he made a terrible husband. He was totally unfaithful and there were terrible scenes of jealousy and recrimination.

Nothing could really tame Frank Harris. He was a born rebel and the more he saw of conventional life, the more rebellious he became. He tried to behave like an English gentleman, but the buccaneer always burst through. He could never hold his tongue, restrict his language, or keep his appetites in check.

Married, made to toe the Tory party line and hampered by old-fashioned directors on the *Fortnightly*, he was in a straitjacket. Something had to give. In fact, everything gave at once. His marriage came to an abrupt end when his womanizing became too flagrant. He printed an article supporting anarchy, which gave the directors of the *Fortnightly* a chance to get rid of him, and he proclaimed Gladstone a hypocrite, causing his Tory supporters to resign.

When the dust had settled he vowed he would never work for anybody again. He bought the moribund *Saturday Review*, talked H.G. Wells, Shaw, Max Beerbohm and other brilliant men into writing for him and became, it had to be admitted by even his worst enemies, one of the greatest editors in London.

He was at the peak of his career. He eventually sold the *Review* and married a pretty little Irish girl, 20 years younger than himself, whose name was Helen O'Hara. He always called her Nellie. His constant love affairs, which cost him a fortune, made sure their marriage did not run smoothly. He ventured into publishing again as the editor of *Vanity Fair* but his scandalous blackmailing of public men and his valiant championship of Oscar Wilde offended just about everybody there was to offend. As his friend Oscar put it, 'Frank Harris has been received in all the great houses – once.'

He rapidly descended the editorial ladder till he was editing a women's magazine called *Hearth and Home* and when that cosy publication failed, he took over *Modern Society*, a publication that depended wholly on gossip and scandal. One of the paper's comments on a co-respondent in a divorce case got him into trouble and he was sent to prison for contempt of court. He raged against everybody and an ill-timed pro-German outburst at the beginning of the First World War in 1914 caused most people in England to turn against him.

Only one man among the literary giants stood by him – Shaw. He knew how Harris loved to shock, and he seemed to have an affection for him. Hesketh Pearson wrote to him all through the war when he exiled himself to America. 'Frank is neither pro-German nor anti-British,' he told those who vilified him. 'He is simply pro-Harris and anti everyone who is not.'

Eventually he got tired of America and longed for Europe. He began to have a great urge to write about his experiences, to record everything, to share his joy in the erotic, to tell it all in minutest detail. 'I am determined to tell the truth about my pilgrimage through this world, the whole truth and nothing but the truth,' he wrote. 'In regard to the body, I go back to pagan ideals, to Eros and Aphrodite . . .'

Perhaps he just wanted to live it all over again. For something terrible had happened. His desire had failed. He was sitting in his New York office one day when a pretty girl passed by his desk. 'For the first time in my life, I was not moved,' he recorded with panic. 'As her slight, graceful figure disappeared, suddenly I realized the wretchedness of my condition in an overwhelming, suffocating wave of bitterness . . . so this was the end; desire was there, but not the driving power. God, what a catastrophe.'

In 1921 he went off to Nice to write that 'dreadful' book. When the first volume of *My Life and Loves* came out it was confiscated if detected in the post. It was surely the most candid autobiography ever written, with every embrace described in language that pulled no punches. Arrogant as ever, Harris saw himself as a martyr.

He contented himself with gallantry towards pretty women in his last few years. Though he pleaded poverty, he managed to live quite comfortably in Nice, sipping his aperitifs in the sun and reminiscing. The day before he died he must have had some premonition that the end was near. He struggled out of bed, seized a glass and hurled it at the wall. It was his last gesture to the world. On August 1931 he died and was buried in the British cemetery in Nice.

Samuel Pepys

On 29 June 1663 Samuel Pepys, handsomely dressed and bewigged, fell into talk with a Mrs Betty Lane. Without much effort, apparently, he persuaded her to accompany him to a Rhenish wine house – 'Where I did give her a lobster and did so towse and feel her all over as to make her believe how fair and good a skin she had; and indeed, she hath a very white thigh and leg, but monstrous fat. When weary I did give over, and somebody, having seen some of our dalliance, called aloud in the street, "Sir, why did you kiss the gentlewoman so?" and flung a stone at the window, which vexed me; but I believe they could not see me towsing her, and so we broke up and went the back way, without being observed, I think.'

So HM King Charles II's Secretary to the Navy Office confided to his diary – the most famous and remarkable diary in the English language, in which Pepys not only painted a vivid picture of his Restoration world in day-to-day detail but also revealed himself as an extremely human, susceptible and lovable man.

His great weakness was for the female sex. That was why he continually made vows that he would improve his behaviour. He lusted after Charles II's mistress, Barbara Palmer, to the extent that the very sight of her smocks and petticoats hanging up to dry in the privy garden at Whitehall filled him with strange rapture. He was always ready to seize whatever pleasure he could find provided always that it was 'attended by safety'. A girl he met in a tavern, pretty and very modest, was fit for three or four quick kisses – 'God forgive me I had a mind to do something more.' A pretty maid coming into the office to fetch a sheet of paper was caressed and kissed. When Becky Allen, a married woman, came up to town she was eagerly desired and offered no opposition. Few women were safe from his fancy – in a 'hot humour' one night he 'soared between wake and sleep into the realms of high treason and sported in fancy with the Queen'.

He met Mrs Betty Lane again one day and took her to The Crown in Palace Yard and there had his full liberty of towsing and tumbling while she 'unabashedly employed her hands about my person to my great content'. As he walked home, in a mighty sweat, he was heartily ashamed and vowed never again would he demean himself. But, according to the diary, a fortnight later he took her on the waters and treated her to a variety of meats and drinks at the Kings Head at Lambeth Marsh and once again was all but carried too far!

Pepys, who has been described as the father of the civil service, began his diary to record the tumultuous happenings going on around him in the winter of 1658–9. He wrote in a neat, slightly sloping hand, in a system of shorthand that he had probably learned at Cambridge. He had no idea he was writing one of the world's most imperishable books. His eyewitness account of Charles II's return from exile, the Plague and the Great Fire of London are all there. But so are his delightful, funny personal encounters. He told his diary nothing but the truth, admitting in extremely comic cod French what he dared not expose to the full light of general knowledge.

Pepys was born on 23 February 1633 right in the lusty, wenching heart of London, above his father's shop overlooking the cobbles of Fleet Street. His father, though a humble London tailor, managed to get him educated at St Paul's School and Cambridge. He married a pretty little French Huguenot when he was 22 and she only 15. He loved her passionately. They lived at first in a little garret in Axe Yard and were very poor. She neglected her household duties to read French romances and he sometimes left her alone too much while he discussed politics in the taverns of Fleet Street or indulged in a little dalliance. But in spite of their difficulties, they were happy enough.

Pepys, with his round face, large, inquiring eyes and clever mind, was soon picked out as a promising young man. In the summer of 1658 he was given a job at the Exchequer. With better prospects he bought himself a good solid house and hired a maid to wait upon them.

A turning point in his life came when Charles II was sent for to restore the monarchy. Lord Sandwich went to The Hague to escort him back to England. And with Lord Sandwich, as secretary, went Samuel Pepys. On his return, he was rewarded by being appointed Clerk of the Acts to the Navy Board.

After that Samuel worked like a demon to improve himself. But he enjoyed so much else in life. He put aside time for the theatre, books and conversation. He loved to dine with great men and listen to their talk, and he loved parties, too. There can be no doubt he entered wholeheartedly into the fun. 'My Lady Penn flung me down upon the bed,' he recorded,' and herself and others, one after the other came down upon me, and very merry we were.' Now there was enough money, he chose his own fine suits and his wife's dresses with greatest care. When at last he could afford to keep his own coach he was the proudest man in London and drove round and round Hyde Park, bowing to his friends.

Samuel's penchant for pretty women showed no sign of diminishing. He believed that provided one did not go too far and was true, in the last resort, to one's wife, there could be no great harm in it. Mrs Pepys was not so sure. She insisted on following her indignant husband round the streets all one afternoon as he 'went about his lawful business'. Fortunately, this time, he did not meet Mrs Betty Lane.

In the year 1664, Pepys reported, he had a 'tempestuous summer of loving', but the fact there was likelihood of War with the Dutch took his mind off wenching. As long as the British fleet was at sea he had great responsibilities. He became tired, sick and sleepless through overwork. One day, in a foul temper, he accused his wife of not being able to control her servants. She answered him crossly and he struck her, only to feel desperately sorry. He hurried off to make her a poultice of butter and parsley. But, increasingly, he found his consolation away from home.

Among his favourites was Jane Welsh, a barber's assistant, for whom he confessed he had a grand passion; Betty Martin, who would sneak home from Westminster Hall with him and in her husband's absence let him do what he would with her and Mrs Bagwell, who in a struggle to preserve her virtue strained his forefinger one day so that it was 'in mighty pain'.

When, however, he was raised to the highest administrative position in the Navy, he made a vow to reform. His resolution did not last very long. The year 1665 brought with it war and the plague and though Pepys was only too aware of 'the solemnity of the times', he seized the opportunity of a wedding in the country to soothe his shattered nerves. Sending for his maid, Susan, to comb his hair he 'nuper ponendo mas mains in sudes choses de son breast, mais, il faut que je leave it lest it bring me to alcun major inconvenience'.

Probably the most shattering experience in his life was the Fire of London in the summer of 1666. He was wakened at three in the morning to be told by his maid, Jane Birch, that a fire had started in the city. He went to the window to look out and judged it to be at the back of Mark Lane. After watching for a while he went back to bed. Next morning Jane told him that 300 houses had burned in the night and the fire was raging along the steep slope of Fish Street. Before the day was out he wrote, 'As far as we could see up the hill of the city a most horrid, malicious and bloody flame engulfed steeples, churches and houses . . . it made me weep to see it.' At four o'clock the following morning he piled his goods into a cart and, dressed only in a nightshirt, set out for Bethnal Green to seek sanctuary with a friend.

With the nation reeling under the twin blows of plague and fire, poor Pepys had to beg for money for the Navy Office. The whole business wore him out but he consoled himself with Mrs Knepp, an enchanting little actress he had been watching for some time. He invited her to dinner, which made Mrs Pepys 'mighty pettish' and when Mrs Knepp felt faint and had to retire to a bedroom, Pepys lay on the bed singing to her and stroking her breasts! When his wife took a holiday in the country he collected Mrs Knepp from the theatre and drove her out in a carriage. He took her to the Tower to see the lions and regaled her with lobster and wine. But it was no use. Though she did not oppose his advances, he dare not venture too far.

So Pepys went on recording the pleasures and pains of his life in careful detail. But by the autumn of 1668 his entries were getting shorter and shorter. For some time his eyes had been causing him great worry. He gained relief for a time by using a pair of spectacles made of paper and soft leather, but he was saddened by the realization that eventually he would have to stop writing the diary he loved.

Towards the end he records a hilarious moment when his wife 'occasioned me the greatest sorrow that I have ever known in this world' by coming upon him with his hand exploring under her maid's petticoats. At the first glimpse of 'that revealing sight' she was struck dumb. Then for the next six months she never stopped berating him, even waking him in the middle of the night to threaten him. Those seeing him in all his finery at the Admiralty during the day would never have believed it.

Pepys made his last entry on 31 May 1669 asking God to prepare him for the ordeal of blindness. But happily his eyes recovered. He never wrote a diary on the same scale again, so we shall never know whether he continued to pursue every woman he fancied. One suspects that he did!

Chapter
Eight

COURTESANS

La Belle Otéro

Her gypsy blood made her different from all the other courtesans in Paris during the Belle Epoque which followed the fall of the Second Empire in France. Dark, golden-skinned and fiery, La Belle Otéro, as she was called, had a temperament so sensational that even kings and emperors dealt with her warily.

Men committed suicide over her, several fought duels, others were ruined financially. She was one of the most acquisitive courtesans of all time and wildly jealous. Though she demanded the freedom to have as many lovers as she wanted, she would fly into jealous rages if those who were paying for her favours so much as looked at another woman.

Otéro has been called the last of the 'grandes horizontales'. She took her first lover in 1880 when she was 12 and she was still striking enough to make people turn and look at her in 1965, the year she died, aged 97.

Proud of her Spanish gypsy strain, she made the most of it. One of the most striking pictures taken of her shows her exquisite hourglass figure encased in a matador 'suit of lights'. She danced in flame-coloured Spanish skirts, slit to show a slender, black silk leg; in the days of her great wealth, like all the courtesans, she sparkled with diamonds under her silk Spanish shawls.

Before she was 20 she was a wild success both as a dancer and as a coquette. Passionate and impulsive, it was nothing for her to jump on a table at Maxim's and dance a fandango so sensual that every man in the room felt she was making love to him. When she added to that excitement the finesse of a practised courtesan she proved irresistible to half the crowned heads of the world.

Grand Duke Nicholas of Russia called her 'Ninotchka' – he was her favourite lover as well as being the most generous. Parisians gave her the name 'La Belle Otéro', by which she became famous. But she was born Augustina Carolina Otéro in the little village of Puentavalga, near Cadiz, on 20 December 1868.

Her mother, Carmencita Otéro was a gypsy dancer who lived in a caravan and performed in the steamy cantinas of Cadiz. One night a Greek ship put into port, its officers went seeking entertainment and one of them, Gregorios Karassou, saw Carmencita and became deeply infatuated. He pursued her, but she would have nothing to do with him. His ship sailed, but a few months later he returned with a Spanish-speaking friend to plead for him. Only when he satisfied her greed for possessions would she become his mistress. He bought a hacienda outside Cadiz and during the next seven years she bore him two sons and twin daughters, one of whom, Carolina, inherited her mother's beauty.

The gypsy grew restless and began to take other lovers, one of them a French winegrower from Cette. Their relationship became so flagrant that Karassou was forced to challenge the Frenchman to a duel. The Greek was killed and Carmencita married the winegrower. Carolina, who had loved her father, hated him and soon her mother, ridden with guilt, could stand her presence no longer and packed her off to boarding school. She would not contribute one peseta towards Carolina's education. The future favourite of kings had to pay for it by scrubbing floors, washing dishes and waiting on fellow pupils.

After about a year, one of the teachers surprised her dancing stark naked on the desks before a crowd of cheering boys. Though only 12 she had the figure of an 18-year-old and was incredibly lovely. One of these boys, called Paco, persuaded her to elope to Lisbon with him where they became lovers. Carmencita found out where she was and had her brought home under police escort. The furious girl ran back to Lisbon, but Paco had disappeared.

Alone, her money running out, she became alarmed. But an amazing stroke of good fortune saved her and set her on the road to success. She used to sing Spanish songs to herself in the room of her hotel. In the room next door the artistic director of Lisbon's Avenida Theatre, staying there while his home was being decorated, heard her and was enchanted. He offered her a contract.

Otéro was a dazzling success, performing in whirling skirts to the click of castanets. Though still under age, she soon had her first lover, a banker, who bought her her first diamonds and established her in a luxurious suite of rooms. But he insisted she gave up the stage and before long she was bored. Hearing that Paco had left Lisbon for Barcelona, she wrote a note of thanks to her patron, packed her bags, gathered up her diamonds and went after him.

She discovered him at the Palais de Crystal, where all the fashionable men of the city hung about, watching performances of light opera on stage and playing the tables for high stakes. Otéro in her Lisbon diamonds and flame-coloured silk attracted their admiring curiosity as soon as she appeared. Paco, astonished but pleased to see his old love in such brilliant style, used his influence to get her a part in a frothy operetta called *Le Voyage en Suisse* at three times the salary she had earned before, and he introduced her to gambling. It became a lifelong passion.

Maturing swiftly, she soon jettisoned Paco for a handsome Italian opera singer, Count Luigi Guglielmo, to whom she was madly attracted. She married him, only to discover he was a philanderer and spendthrift. He took his child bride to the Casino at Monte Carlo and there in 1881 lost the little money he possessed. Night after night he returned, gambling away her savings and even her jewels. Otéro decided she herself would try her luck at the roulette table. Idly, she risked two louis on the red. She lost, and the croupier raked in her money. She went in search of her husband, could not find him, and eventually returned to the original roulette table where she had placed her louis. The croupier, it seems, had made a mistake and unknown to her had replaced her money on the red. An old gentleman touched her arm. 'Madamoiselle would be wise to tempt fortune no longer,' he whispered. The red had come up twenty-eight times. She had won over 50,000 francs.

Though she forgave her Italian count, lived with him in Marseilles and took him with her to Paris, her eyes were on the higher stakes, that would give her the sort of life she craved. Luigi crept away one night and she never saw him again. She was too dazzled by Paris and its possibilities to care. It was 1889, she was 18 and she had experienced more already than most women do in a lifetime.

She was given a contract at the Cirque d'Eté and her debut in the spring of 1890 made her a star. The next day *Figaro* raved about La Señorita Otéro, supple as a panther in her Spanish finery. Admirers began to queue at her door. The great Duc d'Aumale, once the lover of Cora Pearl, took her to his bed. She knew well enough that the great courtesans, whose ranks she was planning to join, made sure they were rewarded by the finest jewels their lovers could afford. Otéro accepted diamonds from the Duc to replenish her collection.

From the start she caught the eye of the great connoisseurs of feminine beauty. The French writer Colette, who admired her, described her in her prime: 'She has the classic profile of a Greek statue: features without a fault, a low and pure forehead. Her nose and mouth are perfectly formed. Her hands and feet are small. Her bosom is white and beautiful. Her breasts are of an unusual shape – they resembled elongated lemons, firm and uplifted.' Barons, princes and dukes paid court to her. She moved around constantly living and performing first in one capital, then another, though always returning to Paris. While in Berlin, for instance, a millionaire banker, Baron Ollstreder, fell in love with her, set her up in a town house with servants, carriages, horses and every conceivable luxury, and in Paris she was never without a splendid villa paid for by some admirer.'

Her lovers became more illustrious as the years went by. In turn she became mistress of two Grand Dukes of Russia, the Tsar, the Prince of Wales, Kaiser Wilhelm of Germany, King Leopold of the Belgians and King Alfonso of Spain.

Her first Russian lover was the Grand Duke Peter, son of Nicholas I, who showered her with jewels and pleaded, 'Ruin me if you like, but never, never leave me.' But she also became mistress of his elder brother, the Grand Duke Nicholas, Viceroy of the Caucasus. Even Nicholas II, the last Tsar, entertained her at clandestine suppers before his engagement to Princess Alix of Hesse.

Otéro first met the Prince of Wales at Marienbad, where he had gone to take the waters. She remembered him as an unfailingly kind and generous lover, who persisted in smoking large black cigars while they dined.

She always said she was afraid of the Kaiser. 'He had such strange, piercing eyes and I could not understand him.' He called her 'meine kleine Wildling', my little savage. He had to be flattered the whole time and his rage was notorious. One night she committed a *faux pas* that meant the end of her relationship with him. She made a careless but not unkind remark about his withered arm. His eyes blazed. 'Out you go,' he yelled. The valet came in to escort her and she curtsied her way out of his presence with all the dignity she could muster.

Her collection of jewels became notorious, and she was sometimes accused of greed because of her passion for them. But they were part of her stock in trade as a courtesan, to show how successful she had been, how grand and wealthy her lovers. She had a waistcoat embroidered back and front with 240 diamonds of the finest quality. She only wore it on the greatest occasions and otherwise it remained safely in the bank vaults. But on one famous occasion she wore no jewels at all and scored heavily over her great rival Emilienne d'Alençon. While Emilienne sat weighed down with diamonds in her box at the opera, Otéro made her entrance in a black velvet gown, cut low, exposing her beautiful neck entirely bare of ornament. But behind came her maid carrying a small mountain of diamonds, emeralds, rubies and sapphires on a tray!

All her patrons were not royal. When she was 35 she met the American millionaire Vanderbilt. He wooed her with a lavish spending she had not experienced before. He gave her a yacht which she sailed to Monte Carlo. She gambled at the casino with reckless abandon and in one week lost £500,000. When Vanderbilt heard what had happened he offered to buy the yacht back from her for that sum with the promise that it was still hers to use as often as she liked.

She retired in her 50s so that she would be remembered in her full beauty. Her later years were spent in the south of France but she gambled away most of her wealth. When she died at the age of 97 she had only one treasure left: a golden spoon, the last of a set presented to her by the Tsar.

Blanche d'Antigny

She was one of the greatest courtesans in the world, but she brought about her own ruin by falling in love. Blanche d'Antigny, who blazed like a star in the *demi monde* of 19th-century France, was, in fact, the inspiration for Zola's novel *Nana*.

Blanche was the convent-educated mistress of kings and khedives, sultans and shahs, but her love for a singer gave her the greatest happiness she had ever known. It lasted such a short time and brought an end to her life of bejewelled luxury, but through Emile Zola's pen, made her immortal.

Her real name was Marie Ernestine Antigny. She was born in the country, the daughter of a carpenter in the little town of Martizay, near Bourges. She loved the fields and hedgerows and would probably never have left rural France but for a crisis in the family.

Her father suddenly left home to live with another woman and Madame Antigny went off in pursuit. She never found him, but decided to stay in Paris instead of returning to Martizay. She took a post as housekeeper with a gentlewoman called the Marquise de Gallifet who gave her permission to send for her daughter.

The Marquise helped Madame Antigny to send Marie Ernestine to a convent school, where most of the pupils came from rich and noble families. It would have been easy for her, as a simple country girl, to retreat into herself. She did at one time think of being a nun. But instead she set out to learn what she could of poise and good manners from these privileged m'amselles who christened her Blanche because of her milky-white skin.

The Marquise died when Marie was 14 and she had to leave the convent. Her mother found her a job in a draper's shop but this was not the sort of life she envisaged for herself. She wanted fine clothes, luxury, admiration. She was already fully aware of her power to attract men with her emerald-green eyes, pale gold hair and white skin. She yearned for a world in which she would be fully appreciated.

One evening a young admirer took her to the famous gaslit pleasure gardens of Closerie des Lilas where she caught a glimpse of the *beau monde*. She was enchanted by the atmosphere, intoxicated by the wine, the scent of cigars and the music. She danced the can-can with abandon, surrounded by admirers. One of them bought her champagne – and seduced her. A few weeks later she went with him to Bucharest.

From now on she assumed the more aristocratic name of Blanche d'Antigny. After abandoning her lover, who proved tedious, she set out to discover what life could offer her in this new country. She knew there was only one profession open to her that would provide the luxury she craved . . . that of the courtesan. She had no difficulty in making conquests. An Armenian archbishop and a prince were said to be among those who introduced her to high society. But life as a lady of pleasure exhausted her after a time and she became ill. Lying on her lace-trimmed pillows she began to think of Paris.

In 1856, when she was 18, she packed and left for home. Somehow or other she was determined to break into the glamorous world of the Paris *demi monde*. She had no contacts. She would have to do it by her own efforts. First, she allowed herself to be admired riding in the Bois de Boulogne in the most elegant riding habit she could afford. After that she flirted with a journalist who, while he had no money, knew the right people. With his help she got herself taken on as a dancer at the Bal Mabille in the avenue Montaigne. Her final 'galop' in the can-can was as abandoned as when she first danced it in the Closerie des Lilas and people began to ask who she was. They were even more curious when she appeared next at the Théâtre de la Porte Martin as the living statue of La Belle Hélène. Every man in the audience gazed enraptured at the beauty of her figure and she was the talk of Paris.

Soon, instead of the artists and journalists who were her early lovers, she began to receive men whose very presence spoke of wealth and an assured place in society. Her income rose and she was able to move from her rather poor lodgings to an elegant, furnished suite of three rooms, the most elaborate being the bedroom with its four-poster hung with embroidered lace curtains, heavy with the scent of ambergris.

In her beautiful book *The Courtesans*, Joanna Richardson tells how Blanche arranged her day. At eleven in the morning she would install herself on the terrace of the Café de Madrid where perhaps her first lover would meet her and take her to lunch at Bignon's or Tortoni's. After lunch she would go home to dress for a regulation five o'clock drive in the Bois de Boulogne. Since she needed to attract attention, she would hire a handsome coupé in winter, an elegant open carriage in summer. When it was time for absinthe she went to one of two cafés she regularly frequented where she met financiers, writers and actors.

While in her box at the theatre one night in the spring of 1863 she became aware of a dark, handsome man watching her. In the interval he asked to be introduced. He was Russian, and a prince. That night over roses and champagne at the supper table he became so infatuated that he begged to be allowed to set her up in a palace in St Petersburg. But Blanche now had many admirers among the French nobility, including the Vicomte de Turenne, and she was not in a hurry to leave Paris.

The Prince was persistent, however, and when summer came and with it the grand exodus from Paris, she allowed him to take her to Wiesbaden, one of the most fashionable watering places of the era. There she created a sensation with her beautiful colouring, gorgeous clothes and magnificent jewels. She gambled wildly and attended every party in the calendar until the Prince was exhausted and glad to drag her off to Russia at last.

She had no idea what to expect. Her protector settled her into the Hôtel de France while he supervised the furnishing of a handsome house. Within a few weeks she moved into her residence with its fine carpets, magnificent tapestries and silver icons. Attended by her moujiks, her footmen and coachmen, her chef and her maître d'hotel, she received the Prince and his friends. The élite of St

Petersburg would assemble for supper at her house after the theatre.

Perhaps all the adulation went to her head. After four years in Russia she committed a *faux pas* that even a Siberian peasant would have known was dangerous. Though she knew it was totally against the rules of society for a courtesan to attend the traditional gala performance which ended the winter season at the opera, she insisted on going. Even worse, she went in a dress which she had been warned had already been chosen by the Empress. She looked far more beautiful in it than its royal wearer. Next morning Mezentseff, chief of the secret police and one of her Russian lovers, was ordered to expel her.

She returned to Paris in the spring of 1868 with a suitcase full of diamonds and proceeded to wear most of them at once, so that people could see she had not been wasting her time in St Petersburg. She wanted to return to the stage and found a fabulously rich new protector, the banker Raphael Bischoffsheim, to support her. Some of the critics were more impressed by her jewellery than by her acting, for on stage and off, she glittered from head to foot with diamonds. She revelled in possessing them and seldom left them off.

Nevertheless, the composer Hervé asked her to play Frédegonde in the operetta *Chilperio*, a piece of froth now long forgotten. She did so, appearing on stage half-naked in nothing but her diamonds and a sheepskin! Following that she created the role of Marguerite in his light opera *Le Petit Faust*, looking, he thought, exactly like a golden-haired Rubens. These two parts established her as a star on the Paris stage.

As her fame increased so did the wealth and status of her lovers. They included royalty and heads of state as well as powerful industrialists and business men. In order to receive them properly she rented a charming house in the avenue de Friedland which she decorated and furnished richly. Her lovers were received by liveried footmen and led to a salon fragrant with hothouse flowers, hung with rich tapestries, royal blue velvet and crystal chandeliers. She would lead them into an oriental smoking room, furnished with low red lacquered tables, encrusted with silver and mother of pearl, where they would be offered exotic cigarettes, cigars and tobaccos from gold boxes. The fortunate ones would progress to the lovers' boudoir, softly-lit and furnished with deeply cushioned divans, or to her bedroom with its enormous four-poster hung with blue silk.

Blanche set the style with great panache. Paris talked of her fabulous dinners at which Bischoffsheim presided, of her bath, made of finest Carrara marble which she filled with two hundred bottles of mineral water, which she found reviving, and of the smart little Russian carriage which she had brought back from St Petersburg.

She was on tour with a play when the Franco-Prussian War broke out. She hurried back to Paris and was there for the siege, turning her beautiful house into a hospital where forty Breton sailors were cared for at her expense. She looked after them herself, earning their adoration. After the war ended and they returned home, some of them sent her gifts of produce from Brittany, begging her to give their greetings 'to all your husbands'.

But the fall of the Second Empire also unleashed fear and violence among people and, quite irrationally, they turned on the courtesans, blaming them for sapping the nation's moral fibre. When the bombardment of Paris began, Blanche had to seek protection from the police. Her parties and gay receptions were condemned as wicked in the face of so much suffering.

When the siege ended she went back to the theatre with relief. But now, at the Folies Dramatiques, she fell deeply in love for the first and only time in her life. The man who won her heart, and who loved her in return, was a tenor known simply as 'Luce'. He had performed with her in *Le Petit Faust* and now their tender relationship gradually took over her life. Luce was not a handsome man; he was short and inclined to stoutness. But his love gave her the greatest happiness she had ever known. Early in 1873 he died of TB and she was heartbroken. She asked for an advance on her wages from the director of the Folies so that she could give him a decent funeral. With delicacy she explained she did not want to bury Luce with money she had earned in bed.

When she fell truly in love she could no longer bear the presence of her official lover, Bischoffsheim, and dismissed him. He never forgave her, and without his support her champagne-filled existence was doomed. Soon the creditors arrived at the house in the avenue de Friedland. They confiscated her carriages, furniture and some of her jewels. She felt the only thing to do was to take flight.

With her maids, her companion Ambroisine, her daughter and coachman Justin, she sailed for Egypt. The director of the Zizinia Theatre, Alexandria, had signed a contract with her for the winter season, paying her almost three times her salary in France. But at her first appearance she was booed off the stage. She left hastily and went to Cairo where the Khedive, who had no doubt at other times appreciated her other talents, received her splendidly. She was persuaded again to return to Alexandria, but her reception was worse than before, and to her horror she found some of her creditors had discovered where she was. She was so afraid of arrest that she entrusted the rest of her jewels to her servants, keeping only a turquoise which Luce had given her. On 28 May 1874, her mother, whom she loved dearly, died. Hounded by creditors and with no home of her own, she booked into a room at the Grand Hôtel du Louvre. Soon after arriving she fell ill with a fever.

Blanche probably brought her death back with her from Egypt. It was either smallpox or typhoid, no one is quite sure which. The horrified manager turned her out of his hotel. Ironically, it was one of her own kind who took her in. The courtesan Caroline Letessier nursed her in her apartment in the Boulevard Haussmann until she died on 28 June 1874. She was not yet 35.

'Skittles'

Every man turned to look as she trotted down Rotten Row in London's Hyde Park. Her figure encased in a riding habit that fitted like a glove, her chestnut hair shining under a rakishly tilted hat, 'Skittles' was a match for every duchess in sight.

Her real name was Catherine Walters. She had come to conquer London from the dingy back streets of Liverpool. She had learned to ride like a duchess, look like a duchess, but she had a voice that 'shattered glass'.

Her amazing success on the London social scene in the 1860s was partly due to her superb seat on a horse, but mostly to the piquant contrast between how she looked and how she sounded. Skittles never lost her Liverpool accent, her native outspokenness or her bawdy sense of humour. That was why she became such a great courtesan. She was different from the rest.

She was born on 13 June 1839 in Henderson Street on the Mersey river front at Liverpool, close by Toxteth docks. Her father worked for HM Customs and had a regular job. Nevertheless, it was a hard world she was born into, tough and uncompromising. There seemed little chance of bettering herself unless she went into service, but while she was a child everyone could see that she was going to be a raving beauty.

When she was old enough she used to earn a few pennies stacking up skittles in the skittle alley at Black Jack's Tavern where her father used to drink. That was undoubtedly where she got her nickname. She matured early, as children did in those circumstances, and probably took her first lover when she was in her early teens.

Then something happened that changed her entire life. Her family moved to Tranmere in the Wirral, Cheshire. She was introduced for the first time to hunting country, the chase, beautiful thoroughbred horses and fine horsemen. She probably worked at a livery stables or those attached to an inn where the local Hunt met. Somehow she was taught to ride, and to ride well.

Society people from London would come up to Cheshire for the hunt and she was fascinated by them. She began to look askance at local boys and told herself that one day she would have an elegant lover with fine manners. Sooner or later, as Henry Blyth says in his biography of Skittles, it was inevitable that she should find her way to London, following in the footsteps of the society people who, at the end of the hunting season, went back to their houses in Mayfair.

She was 20 when she headed south and she found the London of the 1860s an intoxicating place. She drifted into taking the odd lover to keep herself and frequented the Argyll Rooms, beloved by army subalterns, where she thrived on the gay, noisy, permissive atmosphere.

After a few months she was introduced, by chance, to the owner of a prosperous livery stable in Bruton Mews, off Berkeley Square. She may well have spent the night with him. She was longing to go riding in the park and he could provide her with the sort of hack she could not otherwise afford. Skittles had watched the upper crust on display in Rotten Row and the Ladies' Mile, which separated Apsley House from Kensington Palace. Here could be seen the best riders in Britain, the finest horses, the cream of society. It was no place for novices. But she wanted to try.

By now she was earning a reasonable living and the owner of the stables was impressed by her style and elegance. He offered to mount her on the best horses in his stables, to allow her to drive the finest and most expensive little phaetons, then he took her to an exclusive tailor to have her fitted out in the most expensive habit, made all in one piece so that it fitted her like a glove.

They made a deal. She would be required to ride through the park each day to show off his horses. He would see she was fitted out.

No one riding in the park that spring of 1861 looked prettier. She even gained her first touch of fame. Sir Edwin Landseer, renowned for his animal paintings, used her as a model in his picture 'The Taming of the Shrew' in which a beautiful young woman is seen subduing a mettlesome mare.

One day, about a year later, Skittles, trotting happily through banks of spring daffodils saw 'the greatest prize in London' coming on horseback towards her. Lord Hartington, 28, eldest son of the Duke of Devonshire and a bachelor, raised his hat, and what happened next no one is quite certain. Did she fall? Did she faint? Did he save her life as the horse bolted? Whatever happened, Skittles returned to the stables on the arm of 'Harty Tarty'. And the next thing London knew was that she was having a passionate affair with him.

Hartington installed her in a fine house in Mayfair with a retinue of servants and as many thoroughbred horses as she wanted. He was not very handsome for he had rather a long face, heavy beard and soulful expression, but they were very much in love. He was unconventional enough to take her to the Derby and be proud of showing her off. Most English aristocrats were more hypocritical about their mistresses and kept them away from society. She was riding on the crest of a wave, the lover of the next Duke of Devonshire. But if she ever entertained ideas that she might be the next duchess, they were soon dispelled.

After a time Hartington began to get restless, perhaps realizing that he was getting too involved. He went off to America to get a first hand view of the Civil War, leaving Skittles with an annuity and a settlement from the Duke of Devonshire.

**Lord Hartington,
later Duke of
Devonshire**

**Catherine Walters,
usually known as 'Skittles'**

She had her next major affair in Paris. Out of love with London, she crossed the Channel to try her equestrian skill in the Bois de Boulogne. The displays there were just as elegant as in Rotten Row. When she first appeared in a royal blue habit, so close fitting it was said to have been stitched on to her while she stood naked, she created a sensation.

Watching closely as she played the field was a shrewd, intelligent man of the world, 63-year-old financier Achille Fould, Jewish, a man of taste, culture and wide interests, he had been French Minister of Finance five times. The more flamboyant courtesans did not interest him, but Skittles did. She amused and intrigued him. He enjoyed the possibility of turning her into a *grande dame*. He tried to stop her swearing, interested her in the arts, talked to her about pictures and encouraged her to read. She enjoyed his smooth sophistication and he bought her the most expensive thoroughbreds to ride.

Under his guidance she surrounded herself with a small but select group of wealthy and influential people. She did not try to copy the grand salons of the great courtesans in Paris. Her tastes were simpler and, quite naturally, more refined. She rode daily in the Bois, then gave select parties, laid out with the finest crystal and china, in the evening.

It was in France that she first met the poet Wilfrid Scawen Blunt, a handsome, wild-eyed young man, then in the diplomatic service. She was his first mistress and he never forgot the few days of passion they shared. She glimpsed with him a hint of what true love would be like. The experience made her sparkle; it made him suffer. Temperamentally, they were light years apart. Realizing his brooding, romantic nature would eventually drive her mad, she left him to his tears. When he recovered, they became lifelong friends. For a long time after this she avoided younger men, determined never again to become emotionally involved.

Skittles loved hunting and first appeared on the hunting field in 1861 when she hunted in Leicestershire with the Quorn. Some of the women thought the presence of a 'London whore' an insult. But, in fact, she behaved very discreetly, putting up at the Haycock Hotel at Wansford, near Market Harborough, and troubling nobody to entertain her. She was the only woman to go over the jumps at the National Hunt Steeplechase and the men cheered her to the echo.

When in London she held Sunday salons at her house in Chesterfield Street where one of her famous visitors was William Ewart Gladstone, then leader of the House of Commons. They had been introduced one afternoon in the park by Wilfrid Blunt and found a common interest in horses. Gladstone asked Skittles 'about her childhood in Liverpool'. He was then in his 50s. His enemies called him a crank and his admirers, a saint, as he went out on the streets of London, trying to save 'fallen women'. He did not appear to have made any attempt to save Skittles. She was always shocked and angry at any suggestion they were lovers. They were very good friends.

Edward VII loved her tea parties with wafer-thin cucumber sandwiches, big creamy cakes and roaring fires in winter. He said he went there to hear the latest gossip. She probably became his mistress but he certainly enjoyed her company and her earthy good humour. Wisely, Skittles cultivated friendship, for she knew that while lovers could vanish with her looks, friends she could keep.

Her nose was put out when the Empress Elizabeth of Austria came to England. The Empress was just as great a horsewoman as Catherine Walters, and a dashing figure. Her feats in the saddle became legendary. Skittles accepted that her heyday was over with the 80s and settled comfortably at a house in South Street, Mayfair, where her old lover, Wilfred Blunt, now married to an heiress and turned Arabic, came to see her along with the Prince of Wales and others.

Quite suddenly she became Mrs Alexander Horatio Baillie and wore a gold ring on her wedding finger. Her husband, it emerged, was a friend of the Prince of Wales and his family had had close connections with Lord Nelson. He was a tall, handsome Edwardian gentleman, just the sort she had always admired. Perhaps she had really joined the upper crust at last. But when she died on 4 August 1920 the sad truth came out. She was named on the death certificate as 'spinster of this parish'.